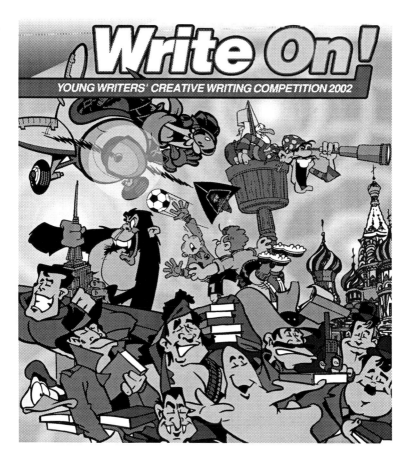

NORTHERN SCOTLAND

Edited by Claire Tupholme

First published in Great Britain in 2003 by
YOUNG WRITERS
Remus House,
Coltsfoot Drive,
Peterborough, PE2 9JX
Telephone (01733) 890066

HB ISBN 0 75434 173 9
SB ISBN 0 75434 174 7

FOREWORD

This year, Young Writers proudly presents a showcase of the best short stories and creative writing from today's up-and-coming writers.

We set the challenge of writing for one of our four themes - 'General Short Stories', 'Ghost Stories', 'Tales With A Twist' and 'A Day In The Life Of . . .'. The effort and imagination expressed by each individual writer was more than impressive and made selecting entries an enjoyable, yet demanding, task.

Write On! Northern Scotland is a collection that we feel you are sure to enjoy - featuring the very best young authors of the future. Their hard work and enthusiasm clearly shines within these pages, highlighting the achievement each story represents.

We hope you are as pleased with the final selection as we are and that you will continue to enjoy this special collection for many years to come.

CONTENTS

The Stories

THE MIDNIGHT CALLER

One dark, stormy night while I was sleeping, I heard a loud *Bang!* I quickly jumped out of my bed and woke my friend Samantha Murdoch. We ran down the stairs very quickly keeping close together because we were scared. Samantha was bursting for the toilet so she went to the loo and I stood outside the bathroom door waiting for her to come out.

She was taking too long, so I said, 'Can you hurry up in there?'
There was no answer. I got really scared so I tried the door slowly. It opened and I went right into the room, but there was no sign of her anywhere. A cold breeze filled the little bathroom. I looked up and saw that the window was open. She has escaped I said to myself. Then I heard a very loud *Bang!*

I heard a creepy, deep voice so I went to run up the stairs and three sharp knives came flying at me. They all hit me on my back. I fell to the ground, but just managed to see who it was. They had an invisible cloak on. The person took it off and left it lying on the ground. The door swung open and the wind was blowing everything about.

The next morning I found myself lying on the settee with my mum sitting beside me. I asked her why I was lying there. My mum said when she was coming down the stairs she found me lying there so she picked me up and put me on the settee then phoned the doctor to come out.
'How did you manage to get there in the first place?' she said. So I told her the story.

Louise Burns (11)
Alyth Primary School, Alyth

TIC-TAC-TOE DARES

'It's your shot Callum, announced Shane.

'OK, OK.'

Callum went to take a good shot, but decided to take a risk. Shane saw how he could win and took his shot.

'I won, wahoo, too bad Callum. I dare you to go to the haunted house at the end of Deal Grove.'

'But.'

'Are you scared, a wee chicken.'

'Where's Deal Grove?' asked Callum hesitantly.

Shane pointed to the sign that said *Deal Grove*, Callum took a gulp, stood up and walked to the sign. He looked up and saw where the arrow was pointing. It pointed to a dusty road with a boarded up house at the end. Callum started strolling towards the house with Greg and Shane following him.

Callum reached the house. He walked up the creaky, wooden stairs across the broken decking to the battered door. He reached for the doorknob. His hand turned numb. He touched the knob, but couldn't feel it. As he grasped the knob Greg and Shane stepped back, but Callum carried on. He twisted the handle, pushed the door open and crept in. As he let go of the door it closed right behind him.

He heard something up the stairs. Somehow his fear was gone, so he walked up to the bottom of the stairs, looked up and saw . . .

Greg Macintyre (11)
Alyth Primary School, Alyth

2

A FRIENDLY GHOST STORY

Once upon a time there was a little girl called Sally. Sally lived in a big house in the country with her mum and dad. Sally's mum and dad worked all the time and Sally spent a lot of time on her own with only the housekeeper and maid for company and even they were too busy to bother with her.

The house that Sally and her family lived in was large and rambling. There were lots and lots of large rooms. Sally's bedroom was on the second floor and was very big, but it was pretty and full of lots of her toys. But Sally kept losing things around the house.

One night at bedtime Sally couldn't find her favourite doll. She looked all around her room but could not find it. She thought she heard a noise outside in the hall and ran out to see if her mum and dad had come home, but there was nothing there. Further down the hall a door closed. Sally crept down the hall and opened the door that she had heard closing and there, in the middle of the floor, was her doll - in a room she wasn't allowed in, so how had her doll gotten there?

As she closed the door she felt a wind go past her. She turned round to see who was there, but there was no one in sight. She was beginning to get scared now so she made her way back to her bedroom. When she got there she opened her door and there sitting on the bed or floating above the bed was the funniest looking, fat, little ghost. Sally stood completely still - she couldn't believe her eyes. She did not feel scared because the ghost was smiling at her. All around the ghost were all the toys Sally had ever lost. The ghost had been hiding them.

Now Sally wasn't lonely any more, because she had her friendly ghost to play with and they played hide-and-seek with Sally's toys. Their favourite game was to frighten the housekeeper and the maid by moving things around.

Lynda Murdoch (11)
Alyth Primary School, Alyth

The Unexpected Guest

There were two school chums who were called Olivia and Natasha who sometimes wrote silly notes to each other, just for fun. The notes were often full of suggestions for pranks of one kind or another. They had been best friends since they first met up as four-year-olds in the same nursery. They were now in their first year of High School, enjoying feeling all grown-up, carrying their books from class to class through the huge, never-ending corridors, giggling as they frequently got lost, only to arrive red-faced and breathless at their next class.

They had made new friends too. There was Shelly, with her long, blonde hair and large blue eyes. How Olivia envied her looks. Then there was Natalie, though Olivia couldn't quite make her mind up about her yet.

The four friends had planned to go on a holiday to Edinburgh. They had it all planned. They were leaving on the Friday after school and would stay with Natasha's mum because she lives with her dad in Dundee.

The first day was the Saturday. The girls had planned to go to the Butterfly and Insect Park. They did not notice they had an unexpected guest.

That night when they came home they saw the guest. It was a ghost. The girls ran all the way home and Natasha's mum found out that the ghost was Natasha's dad in a white quilt sheet.

Emma Arnott (11)
Alyth Primary School, Alyth

THE MANSION

In Scotland, in the darkest forest, there was a mansion. Now, this was no ordinary mansion, it was the biggest one in the UK and it was all covered in ivy and mud. There was mist in the air, which made it even spookier for James, who was a tourist just visiting Scotland to see the mansion.

His journey was from the south of England to the north of Scotland to see the mansion and find out about it, but it looked uglier than the photograph and he was not sure that he was at the right house. Just then he saw something through the mist which looked like a pair of eyes glowing. The pair of eyes were huge and red in colour. He was transfixed by the eyes when suddenly he realised they were coming towards him at very high speed. James began to run for the mansion. While he was running, he looked back and saw four huge paws, a massive jaw and those glowing, red eyes. Suddenly he tripped over a tree root that he hadn't seen and cut his leg. James struggled to his feet and hobbled on to the mansion.

As he hobbled onto the doorstep the creature disappeared right in front of him. He looked at his compass to try to find his way out, but it was broken. He thought to himself that it must have broken when he tripped. There was no way out now, he knew it, with his cut leg and the creature out there. He knew he would be lucky to survive the night.

James was never seen again. Some say that they could hear his screams at night and some say it never happened, but we assume that the cat-like creature must have got him.

Gregor McNee (11)
Alyth Primary School, Alyth

ANDY'S DREAM

Andy lay in bed, tossing and turning. He could not stop thinking of home, the fish and chips wrapped in newspaper, playing out in the street for as long as he liked. As he tossed and turned he slipped into a deep sleep.

He was flying above the clouds. His arms stretched out like a bird, then he started to go down. He fell in front of his house. He was home. There was a grand house with Rosie and Nobby inside, a sparkling clean car and, most importantly, his friends playing out in the street. He joined in.

After a while he started to get hungry. Then like magic, his pockets filled with money. He laughed and started to skip merrily to the fish and chip shop. There he bought the biggest portion of chips, wrapped in newspaper, ever. He started to eat faster than ever before and in two seconds flat the chips were gone. He ran outside to play with his friends. They all went down to the park.

After a while all his friends went home, but not Andy. He sat on a swing, swinging gently in the breeze until he found himself rising into the air. He was flying again, but suddenly he was being shaken. He was caught in a storm. Andy woke up. To his relief it was Laura shaking him gently, 'It's time to wake up Andy. Time to get up.'

Danielle Borrett (11)
Alyth Primary School, Alyth

A WHISPER IN THE GRAVEYARD

My footprints track across the faint dew still lying on the grass. My boots crunch heavily on the hard, gravel path and I'm talking to myself as I walk, schoolbag bumping on my back. But the residents lodged on either side won't mind, they're dead - all of them.

I eventually reach my den. I collapse into it and start rummaging about for my secret rations. Ah! Found them, they're in the corner of my den. Oh, what was that? It seemed like the sound of thunder and lightning. I must go home, but I can't. It's school hours and I will get into trouble. Oh no! I think I can hear footsteps. I will creep up to the entrance and look carefully around.

I am afraid, I think I might just have to creep out and hide behind the gravestones until . . . the footsteps are getting closer. I run to the first stone and the second, plus the third. Phew, I think I am far enough away, but am I?

I can hear a voice, maybe I should go back to the school and tell Mrs Cramp that . . .

Someone is speaking, they are saying to me, 'Go back to school.' But I didn't hear the rest because . . .

Catherine Gordon (11)
Alyth Primary School, Alyth

RUNAWAY

My heart was beating fast. My breath was becoming sharper by the second. My golden hair was getting tangled in the fir tree branches. I had to jump over logs, leap over ditches and dodge little divots in the ground. I felt lost and alone in the middle of nowhere. I wanted to go home. Trees enclosed around me. I felt as if I was running round in circles. The wind stung my face like a thousand bees. Beads of sweat were beginning to pour down my face. I could also feel my T-shirt sticking to my back. I was starting to think that I would never find my way home!

I was walking very slowly. A voice in my head said calm down Alex, just calm down, so I did. I am very asthmatic and stupidly forgotten to take my inhaler! I could feel my breath getting shorter. I knew I was about to have an asthma attack. I stopped, things started to move, I couldn't breathe. I needed my inhaler fast! Otherwise something serious could happen. The next thing I knew everything was pitch-black and I could feel the mossy, earthy ground beneath me.

I woke with a start. I held my inhaler in my hand. I don't need this I thought, 'It was all just a nightmare,' I said with a sigh.

Rachel Mitchell (11)
Alyth Primary School, Alyth

A GHOST STORY

It was one dark night when not a soul could be seen and not a single sound could be heard, until something jumped out of a bush. Then Evan, the little girl who stayed in the house surrounded by bushes, jumped out of her bed as fast as she could and looked out of her window. No one was to be seen. As she turned around to go back to her bed, there were five little, slimy, ugly creatures all standing in a line that they thought was straight, but it was just a horrible mess.

'What are you?'
'You mean who are we?'
'Sorry, who are you?'
'We're the goblins from Planet X.'
'Where's that?'
'We can't say, and anyway we shouldn't be talking to you like this.'
'But why?'
'Because.'
'Because what?'
'Because we are just not allowed. Now listen, we have a challenge for you. If you want your family back you're going to have to complete a labyrinth.'
'What do you mean?'
'We mean you must complete a labyrinth to get back your family.'

Evan waits for a minute with only thirty seconds to think. 'I've got it, I'll risk the challenge on one condition.'
'Yes.'
'You give me more than three days to do it and a bed and pillow to sleep on at night and they must be comfy.'
'Okay, that's a deal!'

So as she set off with a bag on her back she finally reached the labyrinth and as she opened the door she saw . . .

Serena Alexander (11)
Alyth Primary School, Alyth

A Day In The Life Of A Horse

'I'm going to see the Miller's new horse tonight after school!' said Sarah excitedly as she sat down to eat lunch with her friends. The Miller's were good friends of her parents.

'I heard that horse was magic!' said Mary.

'How would anyone know? They just moved here!' They had recently moved to Civlian Town from a place in England called Boser. Sarah's parents were very happy for them to be back so they were visiting them tonight.

The minute the bell rang Sarah was out of school and home before the teacher could dismiss the class! She quickly shoved an old pair of jeans, a scruffy top and her wellies into a bag, then hopped on her bike and went to meet her parents before rushing off to meet the horse.

Once she arrived at the Millers the oldest daughter Rachel showed her the stunning grey horse. Immediately she fell in love with it. 'She's beautiful! What's her name?' asked Sarah.

'Molly. It's plain, but it suits her.'

'Molly,' repeated Sarah, 'it's lovely.'

'Would you like to ride her?' said Rachel.

'Yes please!'

So the two girls took Molly in from the field before grooming and tacking her up.

Once the girls had ridden they brought Molly to her stable and rubbed her down.

'I've got to go. Do you mind seeing that she goes back out to the field?'

'Not at all,' said Sarah eagerly. But as she was taking her out something terrible happened. Molly reared and came crashing down, hitting her. She fell to the ground and became unconscious. While there was a frantic going-on Sarah went into a dream. She was Molly galloping about the field. She felt free as the sun shone brightly on her. Then it became colder and started to snow, she was cold and miserable *and then* she was in a cosy stable and was getting groomed and tacked up. Then a child sat on her back and started kicking her, which she didn't like at all!

Suddenly she woke up. She was sweating. 'Where am I?' she asked confused.

Her mother told her the whole story. She decided on one thing, she was glad she wasn't a horse!

Jordan Barclay (11)
Alyth Primary School, Alyth

THE SPOOKS BALL

One cold, winter's night when all the villagers were sleeping, a light in the house on haunted hill went on and two skeletons stood chatting until a witch in hideous rags asked one of the skeletons to dance. There were many spooks dancing. Ghosts danced with ghouls, vampires and werewolves.

They were all having a good time until they noticed someone peering in the window. Someone shouted, 'Catch him.'
At that point the man who could not believe his eyes at what he had seen turned to run. But one of the spooks was running towards him so he tried to run the opposite way, but found his way blocked. The window of the house was open so he pulled himself up and inside the house. He ran left, right, upstairs and down.

Eventually he found a place to hide, it was a cupboard full of sheets. Suddenly he had an idea, he would put the sheet over himself and pretend to be a ghost. As he tried to get out, the door was locked. He leaned against the door and fell though with an almighty thump.

The man walked slowly. While he was walking, the end of the sheet got caught and fell off. All the spooks were chasing him. He shouted, 'Please don't hurt me.'
His wife woke him and said, 'You're having a bad dream.'
He tried to get up, but he was tangled in the sheets. Was it a dream?

Rebecca Crabb (11)
Alyth Primary School, Alyth

DRIPPING GUTS

One night Callum phoned his two friends Shane and Brian and asked if they wanted to stay the night. They both came round.
They were watching a scary movie and later on they started telling each other ghost stories. They started getting freaked out and then started playing dares. They all wanted to have a midnight feast, but it wasn't quite 12 o'clock. They went down the stairs and got sweets and crisps while Callum's mum and dad were in bed sleeping. While they were downstairs, Callum went to the toilet and Shane and Brian went back upstairs.

Early the next morning at about 4 o'clock while it was still dark they heard a dripping noise and started getting the shivers down their backs. About an hour later after talking to each other to keep one another company they decided to go downstairs to watch the football. They had to be careful not to wake up Callum's brother, mum and dad, even though it was their favourite teams playing.

They heard a tap dripping so they searched upstairs and downstairs, but no tap was on. They all tried to think where the dripping might be coming from, but didn't know where to look. Brian's idea was to look in the heating cupboard so they tried there, but didn't hear any noises or movements in the house. Callum said, 'I think I'd better wake up Mum, Dad and Frazer.' When Callum had done that, Shane and Brian searched under the sink and all you could hear was a screaming noise. It was a dead dog with blood dripping from it.

All they said was that it was like pins being pushed through you and ever since I've had nightmares.

Samantha Murdoch (11)
Alyth Primary School, Alyth

THE BOY

This story all started one day in May, the year 1985, a May day holiday. There was a boy who thought that he was cool and went on Loyal Hill.

The next few days nobody saw that boy until they found him with ten cuts all over his body.

In 2002 in May I was going up the same hill when I saw a knife on the ground and then I thought of the story I'd heard about the boy on the hill. I changed my mind and I didn't want to go on the hill that day, but when I got up the hill I heard the sound of a person moaning, so I screamed and ran down the hill. I met my mum and Karen and told them what had happened.

When I got to school I looked in the library for the story, but I did not find it. The next day I went up the hill again and heard the same sound, but it didn't scare me this time. The story that I found out was that a boy was found, but he was still alive and you can still hear the boy crying and that was how the boy was found.

Grant Watson (12)
Alyth Primary School, Alyth

A DAY IN THE LIFE OF A HURRICANE PILOT

'The Battle of France is over, the Battle of Britain is about to begin,' Churchill's words echoed through Henry Custer's mind as he ran towards his Hurricane fighter aircraft. On the south side of the airfield explosions, the sound of shrieking bombs, cries from wounded personnel and the gentle humming of German bombers overhead, made the moment very spine-tingling.

Henry scrambled into the Hurricane, yanked back the starter, kicked the brake lever off and sped off down the runway. Once the aircraft had reached the needed take-off speed Henry pulled back the control column and was airborne.

The large, menacing shape of a Messerschmidt flew overhead; Henry pulled his aircraft up and fired 13 rounds at it. He smiled as it spiralled towards Earth. Swinging the plane round he strafed another German bomber. It too suffered the same fate as the previous. He glanced over at it to see the only 2 surviving aircrew jump clear before it smashed into some woodlands, setting the whole 200 acres alight. Twisting the column round he came on the tail of a Messerschmidt fighter, which was gunning down a damaged Spitfire. Henry calmly pulled the trigger and watched as machine gun rounds pounded into the German aircraft until its fuel tanks exploded. One of its shattered, burning wings spinning past him and finally embedding itself in the roof of hangar 19. Henry turned his Hurricane back to base, knowing there would be no more German raiders until tomorrow.

Martin Arnold (12)
Alyth Primary School, Alyth

A NIGHT IN THE LIFE OF A TOOTH FAIRY

Late at night Lea had a tooth fairy mission to complete. She was tired and worn out, but she still had to do it. So small and so weak, she lifted up Zara's pillow and swapped her white, shiny tooth with a £2 coin. Zara felt a tickle down her neck, she immediately woke and screamed. With Leah's ear being so small, Zara's screaming nearly burst her eardrums. She covered them and whispered, 'Why me? Why couldn't I have done Callum's mission? *My* usual human boy.'

Zara turned round and saw Lea, with her wings flapping rapidly. Lea flew into the far corner. By this time Zara had stuck her key into the keyhole, so Lea couldn't get out. Lea was trapped, trapped for the night.

Rosina the tooth fairy queen had tooth radioed Lea to make sure she was alright for she had been out for almost 2 hours, but because she was so frightened all that came out was a short and sweet, 'Go away!' Rosina thought Lea was talking to her so she threw the tooth radio away and said, 'If you need my help, you needn't bother asking for it.' Lea meant to say this to Zara but she got all confused.

'I've got you now!' shouted Zara, as she held Lea in her cupped hands. 'You go away and don't come back!' she screamed as she chucked her out the window.
Phew, thought Lea. I'm glad Zara thought I was some kind of fly.

Emma Mahoney (11)
Alyth Primary School, Alyth

A Day In The Life Of A Caterpillar

On a sunny day in Yorkshire, a caterpillar was crawling along a branch to get some leaves to munch on. He was just about to crunch when someone picked him up. It was a little boy called Callum and before he knew it, he was in a jam jar with a couple of withered leaves, the only good thing was that he had remembered to put holes in the lid.

The caterpillar was then carried home in Callum's careful hands to be shown to his mum. 'Oh Callum,' cried his mum. 'You must let this poor creature back into the garden so he can live his life and progress to freedom.' Callum reluctantly took his new friend into the bushes at the bottom of the garden and said goodbye to the caterpillar.

The caterpillar breathed a sigh of relief when he found himself back where he was, but oh no, where were his friends Kate and Percy? Had they too been taken away in a jar by a huge human? Just as he was beginning to worry he heard a familiar sound. A sound of munch, munch, munch! 'Hooray,' the caterpillar cried as he was reunited with his friends after a stressful day in a caterpillar's life.

Arlene Stewart (11)
Alyth Primary School, Alyth

A DAY IN THE LIFE OF A FARMER

A farmer's day starts very early in the morning especially if he has a herd of dairy cows. The farmer rises early, around 5am, goes out to the field and brings in his herd for milking. He organises all the cows in the large sheds and puts on all the milking machines to do all the milking. From there he puts it into large containers and a tanker lorry comes and picks up the milk to deliver to the creamery who bottle it for the shops etc.

Then the farmer has to feed his cows, sheep, hens and maybe even pigs, before he starts the rest of his jobs for the day, like ploughing, sowing or harvesting, depending on the season of the year.

At other times of the year he will have to get sheep clipped and then he will have a time for selling his sheep and cattle and either take them to the market for selling or hire in a float to take them there for him. The farmer will have to go to the market to watch the auctioneer selling his animals and see if he gets a good price for them.

At the end of the day he will get a well-earned meal and rest and plan what he will do the next day, then set his alarm for 5am again.

Lisa Murison (11)
Alyth Primary School, Alyth

A Day In The Life Of David Beckham

David Beckham woke up about 6 o'clock with excitement. He had a leg massage to loosen up his muscles, because it was sore after the game. Yesterday, the England team flew to Japan for the final. They flew from London airport at 3pm. They flew over the Netherlands, Germany and Holland.

Today David's going to training. They have to run a mile and practise taking corners, free kicks and penalties. Now it is 15 minutes to the final of the World Cup. David goes to say goodbye to Victoria and Brooklyn.

Time for the match. David felt nervous coming through the tunnel. Michael Owen got hacked just before half-time. Then it came to penalties. David scored and so did the Japanese team. David scored the winning goal. So England stand with the World Cup!

Callum Clive (9)
Buchanhaven School, Peterhead

A DAY IN THE LIFE OF LORD VOLDEMORT

Voldemort was relieved to be alive after Harry's spell. But he still had to kill Harry Potter. Even though he was weakened. Voldemort was looking for a unicorn, to suck its blood to stay alive, but he heard someone else walking about. He checked to see who it was and it was Harry Potter. He pounced at Harry and pinned him down to the ground. He said, 'Finally I get to kill you Potter.' Voldemort knocked him out with a punch and then cast his most powerful spell.

When Voldemort thought it was over Harry got back up. So Voldemort did it again and that put Harry down for good. Then Dumbledore came, but he was too late. He saw Voldemort running, so he cast his most powerful spell and killed Voldemort. After Voldemort was killed, Dumbledore went to check on Harry, but he was dead.

The whole school was very sad especially Ron and Hermione, Harry's two best friends. Hagrid was sad too, but a little bit happy because Voldemort was killed.

Every teacher was sad including Professor Snape. All the children were sad apart from Draco Malfoy, he wasn't really bothered about it. That was Voldemort's and Harry's first day back. Not a very good day. They tried their best to bring him back to life but it didn't work. He was known as the boy who lived and the youngest seeker of the century.

Michael Innes (9)
Buchanhaven School, Peterhead

A Day In The Life Of Amorouso

Amorouso woke up very excited because it was the Cup Final. He got up and put his kit on and went to get his breakfast with his other team mates.

They had finished their breakfast and had a wash and then they went on a bus. They arrived at Hampden Park. They were very excited playing for the Cup. Amorouso had a cheesy grin on his face. They were playing against Celtic.

Rangers won the Cup against Celtic. The score was 3-2. Livincan scored at the last minute. The manager was very, very happy. Amorouso said that he would bring the cup back next year.

Gemma Youngson (9)
Buchanhaven School, Peterhead

A DAY IN THE LIFE OF BRITNEY SPEARS

One day Britney was woken by a loud knocking on the door. She remembered it was the day that they were shooting the new video called *I am not a girl, not yet a woman.* She got out of her bed and went to the door, it was the director with a make-up artist. She got taken to make-up and clothes. They made such a fuss over her just to get her perfect.

Once she was ready she was taken to the top of the mountain where they were filming the video. Britney was so scared that she might fall off the mountain. It was being filmed in Canada. She was scared she might mess up the song or do something wrong. She almost went over the edge of the mountain when she sang the end of the song. It took about six or more hours to film it.

Finally they had finished making the video. They played it over to Britney. She said, 'That was magic and frightening, but I loved it.'

Britney went back to her house and there was her family waiting for her. They shouted with excitement, 'Well done Britney.' She almost fainted. Then they all watched the video together, her family loved it too.

Eilidh Thompson (9)
Buchanhaven School, Peterhead

A DAY IN THE LIFE OF DAVID BECKHAM

David Beckham woke up feeling excited because England was playing for the World Cup. He was the captain of England. He said, 'Here we are playing for the World Cup team England. We're going to win.'

David and his team were staying in a hotel in Japan and went straight to the match.

The first match was England against Scotland. England 1, Scotland 0. Then Scotland got one goal and England scored two goals. David Beckham and his team won the World Cup. They were so happy because they'd won. They went home with the Cup and celebrated. David said, 'Magic, we have won the World Cup, yes we have. Remember that tomorrow we are playing Aberdeen. I will be on the pitch first thing. I will score tomorrow.'

David scored from a penalty the next day, England shouted, 'We've won, we've won!'

Aaran Geddes (11)
Buchanhaven School, Peterhead

SNOWY'S DOUBLE SURPRISE!

There was once a sheep called Charlotte who had a yearling lamb called Snowy. One day Snowy was playing outside. His mum called him into the farmyard. She had a big surprise for him. She told him that any minute now she was going to have a lamb! Snowy thought a lamb was just a *sheep* like himself.

Shortly afterwards he heard his mum bleating. He ran to the farm as fast as he could, to see if anything was wrong. When he reached the farm there was a big surprise waiting for him. A little, white, fluffy ball was curled up in a corner of the barn!

Snowy began to feel strange. 'Oh no,' he shouted, 'a baby. If there is a baby I will be left alone while Mum plays with him . . . or her! Maybe she'll call it a cute name - like Woolly.'

An hour went by and all Snowy thought about was how he was going to spend the rest of his life. However, over the months Snowy grew fond of Woolly and they played and played all day together.

Until one day Charlotte called the *boys* to the farm. Didn't they get a surprise!

Sara McCombe (10)
Cliasmol Primary School, Isle Of Harris

ENCHANTED

There was once a good witch called Bella. Bella wasn't a bit evil, she was the opposite. She was very kind. She lived in a cottage in the middle of the countryside with her pet cat, Morris. You would have expected Morris to be black, but he wasn't. He was ginger.

Bella wanted to be human. She didn't want to be a witch. She couldn't talk to humans because she would turn to dust. The cottage she lived in was beautiful. It had flowers all around it. There was one spell Bella could cast on herself that would allow her to talk to humans without turning to dust. It would mean Bella's cottage would disappear. This would have to happen because the cottage would remind her of being a witch. She would also never remember casting any spells!

Bella looked at the spell. She chanted some words. With Morris by her side the spell was cast. There was a bright light and Bella found herself and Morris in a field. She couldn't remember anything except his name!

Bella soon made friends. She got a job, bought a nice cottage and they lived happily ever after.

Heather Macleod (11)
Cliasmol Primary School, Isle Of Harris

BIGFOOT THE CAMP LEADER

I was on my way to breakfast when the dormitory leader, Sam, walked up to me saying that we had to be outside at ten o'clock.
'We're going to walk to the top of the hill,' he explained, pointing at a large hill through the window.

At quarter to ten, very unenthusiastically, I went outside where Marcus, the camp leader, was distributing bags containing maps and compasses. When we were ready we set off.

After a long walk, we arrived back at camp to be told that David, the boy I shared a dormitory with, and Marcus, hadn't been seen since the hill walk. So we had to stay in our dormitories until they were found.

After what seemed hours, we were told that both David and Marcus had been found safe and well . . . apart from the fact that David had somehow got it into his head that *Bigfoot* had kidnapped him!

Nobody believed him, of course, but we all agreed to look for *Bigfoot* just for a laugh! To everyone's surprise we found *Bigfoot*, but on looking closer we realised it was someone dressed up. But who? No! It couldn't be. It was . . . Marcus!

Ruairidh MacKay (11)
Cliasmol Primary School, Isle Of Harris

SOULS AND DEVILS

In the graveyard Tomthom was. He felt scared, he thought there was something weird behind him. He felt a cold, evil touch on his shoulder. He turned around to see who was behind him. It was the soul stealer! This creature had a body made of bones and had a dark cloak on.

The soul stealer took Tomthom to his boss, the Devil. He gave Tomthom a wish for his soul. He wished in his mind that he wanted to escape from the Devil's home. Then after that he saw an axe and quickly chopped the soul stealer's head off.

The Devil used his magical power to grow and then he tried to flatten Tomthom and eat him. Suddenly Tomthom vanished! He was back in the graveyard. The trouble was over for now!

If you feel something behind you, don't turn back or you might be on a monster's menu for dinner.

Joseph Philip (9)
Foveran Primary School, Ellon

THE SCREAM!

Stephanie and her ten-year-old friend Laura set out to the graveyard to put down some flowers. The only way was through the haunted woods. Stephanie and Laura set off through the woods. Then a burnt tree nearly fell on them. Owls were hooting and ghosts were screaming. Creepy animals ran past them, they were scared out of their wits!

Suddenly, blood started pouring out of Laura's mouth. Luckily, Stephanie never noticed. But then, a strange-looking animal (half lion, half ghost) came flying down and knocked Laura over. She was still alive but she couldn't walk and told Stephanie to carry on without her.

Then an owl swooped down from a tree and dropped a note in her hand. She opened it and read, *Beware you're in for a scare.* At that, Stephanie was really scared. She was searching behind every tree in case something or someone was going to hurt her. Eventually, she arrived at the graveyard. She put the flowers on her grandpa's grave. She wanted to get back quickly, so she ran off. She forgot about the letter and all that other stuff.

All of a sudden, Laura jumped out dripping with blood! Stephanie tried to run as fast as she could, but Laura caught up with her. She pushed Stephanie to the ground and dug her fangs into her friend's neck. Stephanie screamed as loud as she could! Laura must have been a vampire.

Stephanie Asher (9)
Foveran Primary School, Ellon

THE HALLOWE'EN HINDER

One morning Aden and his mum were decorating for Hallowe'en when they ran out of banners. 'We'll have to go and get more,' said Aden's mum. So off they went.

When they got to the shopping centre Aden saw his friend, John. They both went back to John's house. Aden stayed for tea. Then he decided to go home. It was pitch-black. He wanted go get home as fast as he could. He chose to cut through Malsh Grove. When he reached the first yew tree, a storm started. Aden ran up to Malsh Mansion, but Lord Galom's wooden cart was gone. In the distance he could see a fire and a glint of gold . . . There was blood on the ground.

Aden opened the oak doors and went in. The scarlet and red carpet was marked with mud. Aden opened the dungeon door and peered in. There were steps that led to the dungeon. He cut himself on a nail. There was a pool of blood on the stretching machine. Lord Galom's chain was on the ground. A coffin sprang open, a zombie with a spear in its head threw the spear at Aden and missed. The zombie fell and shattered.

A torch flickered on. Aden heard the oak doors . . . He woke.
'It was a dream,' said Mum. Or was it?

Johnathan Kain (9)
Foveran Primary School, Ellon

THE SCARY NIGHT

Iona and her mate Kathryn, who were both 9, had been playing together. On the way home Kathryn dared Iona to stay overnight at the graveyard. Iona went home, packed some things and snuck out for the night. She felt very scared because she believed in ghosts, vampires and all that stuff!

A couple of nights before, a murderer had died. People say that bad people come back and kill innocent people at midnight. But Iona bravely went to the graveyard. She wandered about the graves. Looking for somewhere to sleep overnight. Her thoughts were that the murderers might rise from their graves and kill her. She set up her stuff which took a long time to complete, her tent took the longest. 'Argh!' she screamed. She had heard the howling of a werewolf! She started to feel cold and very frightened.

Suddenly she saw something moving through the graveyard. She quickly crawled into her tent and closed it up. Although she was very frightened, she tried to go to sleep when she heard more strange noises. She peeked out of her tent. She saw ghosts rising from the graves and vampires coming in from the woods. They came up to the tent so she quickly crawled out and ran through the graveyard, not knowing where she was going. She looked all around her and she saw ghosts and vampires with blood streaming from their mouths. When she looked in front she saw a . . . a werewolf, it had blood dripping from its mouth.

When Iona saw the blood dripping from the dog's mouth she fell to the ground. She was unconscious. Morning eventually came, the sun rose up into the sky and she woke up. She went back to her camp and packed her stuff. She ran as fast as she could out of the graveyard. She never set foot in the graveyard again.

Iona told everyone, but no one believed her. Ever since that night the ghosts started to haunt her. Every night they tried to kill her until one night . . . a vampire suckcd her blood. All she felt was sharp teeth going into her neck. She screamed for a second, then she fell to the ground. Blood was pouring out of her neck, was she dead . . .? Did the vampire succeed? Was she rescued? What do you think?

Iona McLeod (9)
Foveran Primary School, Ellon

THE HEART STOPPING TALE OF DOOM

One night John was sitting at home, he was reading a letter he got from his friend who was very ill. John thought he would got to see him after a little drink. After his first drink he had another and another and another!

When he set off he was very drunk. Then he said, 'Come here Pepper,' and so he and his dog set off in the dead of the night. They had no light and they could not see anything. They went to the edge of the wood, there was a sign that said *Beware Death Is Near*. John did not care. They were just going past the first fortress when Pepper stopped, John could not see Pepper. There was a loud bark, John stopped and turned. Pepper was cut in half! John jumped and ran to her but she was dead. Blood was all over her. John cried for a short time then went on sadly.

John was miserable and he was not prepared for what happened next . . . He fell right down to rocky ground and he hit his head hard. He woke up an hour later, he started to climb when he saw a baby with thorns in its head. Hags were looking at the baby and John ran for his life. The hags and baby ran after him. John fell down, down, down. He fell into a cage where his wife was lying on the ground with an arrow in her tummy. He ran through the cage and out of that horrible place. Two vampires started to chase him. He thought I am going to die. He ran and screamed!

He turned around and cobras slithered nearer and nearer. He knew doom was near but when he thought things could not get worse, there were living people with axes in their necks. He screamed and screamed again. John had blood and slime on him. Next jumping eyes jumped at him, they all chased him and he ran for his life. He saw a light ahead, it was his friend's house. He ran and opened the door. His friend said, 'John what's the matter? You don't need to tell me. You saw a ghost. There is no such thing.' At the window were the hags, baby, vampires, axe people, cobras and jumping eyes. So was he drunk?

Kathryn Cruickshank (9)
Foveran Primary School, Ellon

HARRIET AND THE VAMPIRES

Harriet was a ten-year-old girl who lived on a farm with her family. One fine night after school, Harriet took Sparky her horse in from the field. There was a wood beside the farm that the little girl loved to go in with Sparky. She set off through the woods but it started to rain, there was thunder in the distance and dark clouds in the sky. The owls were hooting and bats were squeaking. Harriet was frightened but she felt safe with Sparky.

Suddenly a fox jumped out in front of Sparky, it had blood all over its face and its eyes were shining in the moonlight. Sparky got a fright and galloped off. Harriet could not stop the terrified horse. Harriet was lost in the woods and she was alone.

Through the trees, Harriet could see a big light coming from the sky. It seemed to her that the glow was in the graveyard so she decided to go and see what it was. When she got there, she knew straight away that it was vampires and there were people crawling up from the ground!

She was really frightened now and she wanted to go home, suddenly Sparky reappeared and Harriet felt a little better. She mounted her horse and rode on. However, some vampires jumped out and Sparky reared up so high that Harriet fell off and Sparky galloped away again.

Harriet Ross (10)
Foveran Primary School, Ellon

THE CHASE

One night a boy called William had just left his friend's house. It was 10 o'clock at night. It was a full moon and he had just arrived at the forest. He walked and he walked but the forest never seemed to end. He suddenly saw a light and he walked towards it. The light got brighter and brighter.

Suddenly he saw a horrible sight! He saw witches, vampires and the Devil, they were all sitting round a fire eating dead bodies. William quickly ran away but he fell. The witches, vampires and the Devil heard him so they quickly got up and started to chase him. A zombie jumped out at him. The zombie had a rusty knife through his neck.

They were about to catch him so William climbed up a tree to escape. They sat down and waited, the witches, vampires and the Devil eventually fell asleep, William climbed down the tree slowly and quietly. When William reached the ground he ran and he ran. He got out of the forest as fast as he could.

It was still raining but William did not care about the rain. He was in far too much of a hurry!

Norman Campbell (10)
Foveran Primary School, Ellon

THE RIDE INTO DOOM!

He left his house at the strike of midnight, travelling quickly across the floor. He felt tired, sick and drowsy, for the night before he had gone to the bar. He left his wife and his only child, out the door he went to his horse, Molly. Up he hopped onto her back. He pulled the reins and off they went under the pitch-black sky, he started to feel drowsy and he didn't know where he was going. A puddle splashed him in the face as gravel crunched underneath him.

He travelled into the dark, cold woods, it was getting darker by the minute. He passed a fox out a hunting and an owl high up in a tree. He did not care a tiny bit as he just rode on and on. The sky was getting darker still, would the sun ever rise today? He did not know for sure but still he didn't care. He came to the edge of the forest and he travelled onto the road. He came to a little bridge and over it, he rode.

That was the end of him and his horse, he's never been seen again.

Fiona Ferguson (11)
Foveran Primary School, Ellon

31ST OCTOBER

It was the 31st of October 1999, Sam had just left her friend's party 12 miles away from Sam's house. She trotted towards home with her horse, Sandy. As it was a cold night, she took a short cut through the woods, twigs snapped, leaves crackled and the wind whistled.

Suddenly Sandy reared up on her two hind legs, neighed and took off in the opposite direction. Sam got such a fright, she forgot to hold onto the reins tightly and she fell off and landed on the ground with a thump. As she lay there she heard a loud scream, then there was a crackling noise coming from the bushes. Sam turned around and saw a man with a sharp knife. He started to run towards her. She was terrified. She was scared she was going to die.

Sam got up, she was so scared she started to run. She found an open bush and she ran towards it. She stopped to catch her breath. Anxiously she looked over the bush, the strange man was gone. She thought, Where is he? She turned around to the direction of the sound where he was. He stabbed her in the chest . . . she screamed. He left her there to die.

Jenny Bates (12)
Foveran Primary School, Ellon

THE DARK FOREST

One evening I took my dog called Wallace out for a walk and we walked for miles and miles until I found myself in the middle of a forest. It was now getting very dark and I could just see my dog running around. It was starting to get windy and trees were rustling and I was starting to get scared.

I think I got lost because I couldn't find my way out and I kept going round in circles. Wallace had disappeared and by that time, I was really scared. I kept calling on him but he didn't come back.

I sat down on a big tree trunk and I fell asleep. I didn't know how long I was sleeping for but I woke up when I felt Wallace licking my face. I was so glad to see him. As I opened my eyes I could see an old house just in front of me, there was some lights on in the house, so I went up to the door and knocked. The door was open, I shouted hello but no one answered so I went in.

I started to walk around the house looking for someone but no one was there. I sat down on the chair and switched on the TV but just then the living room door slammed shut. When I looked there was no one there, the lights kept going on and off and Wallace started to bark. The floor started creaking and it sounded like someone was walking on it because I could hear footsteps but still no one was there.

I got up and started to walk to the door and opened it and I got a big shock because standing in front of me was a man wearing a long white coat, so I ran as fast as I could and so did Wallace. Wallace wouldn't wait for me and he reached home long before me, since then I haven't been back to the woods.

Michael Sim (11)
Newhills Primary School, Aberdeen

THE HOUSE OF TERROR

A crisp winter morning sunlight streamed through Will's bedroom window. It fell right across his ginger hair and his long pale face with freckles on his cheeks.

He got up and switched on the TV. The news came on and it said there was going to be a thunderstorm. It was his 18th birthday and he was really excited.

After college he was driving home and the thunderstorm came on. His car broke down in the middle of nowhere and there was only one house in sight. It was a big wooden house with one light on. Will thought he would go and ask if it was possible to use their phone. He walked up the road and he thought he heard footsteps behind him. When he looked there was no one there, so he thought it was just his imagination. When he was walking it felt like the road was never-ending.

Finally he got to the gate and pushed it open and walked up the path. He thought he heard the footsteps behind him again but there was nothing there. When he got to the door, he rang the bell but no one answered, so he rang it again but still no one answered. He decided to try the door to see if it was open but when he reached for the handle, it slowly creaked open. He walked in and looked around, there was big portraits of scary people on the walls and a big spiral staircase. He heard a chopping noise so he decided to walk into the room where he thought the noise was coming from and saw an old lady with a big butcher's knife covered in blood, cutting up a very large piece of meat. At least he thought, it was meat until a human head came rolling off the table and landed at his feet.

He ran out the room and headed for the door and tried the handle but it was locked, so he ran up the stairs and when he got to the top he needed his inhaler but as he took it out of his pocket, he accidentally dropped it down the stairs but decided not to go after it as he was too breathless. He walked down the hall and heard screams so he went into a room and there was nothing in it, something was dripping on him, he looked up and there were about 100 or more people hanging from the roof. He ran out and went into the bathroom and was sick.

He stood up and looked out of the window, he gave out a scream and ran as fast as he could out of the room.

He was about to run down the stairs when he realised there was that crazy old lady standing there with an axe. He ran back into another room, at the end of the room was a big window, he ran up to it and tried to open it but it was stuck, so he was looking around the room when the door opened. About 14 people came bursting through it, Will noticed they were all covered in blood, finally he found something hard. He picked it up and smashed the window. He put his head out to the dark mist of the night. Will looked down, it was a long way to the ground, then he felt something hard and cold running up his back. He was too scared to turn around so he jumped out, no matter what but luckily he landed in a bush. Then with all his might he tried to stand up.

He crawled back to his car because he had twisted his ankle. He finally got back to his car but when Will tried to start it up, it was still broken. He waited for a car to go past, he didn't have to wait long for a car and even better, it was the police but when Will looked around, the house was gone.

Craig McHattie (11)
Newhills Primary School, Aberdeen

A DAY IN THE LIFE OF A LIBRARIAN

A few years ago in spring there was a librarian called Mary. Every day she got up, come rain or shine. Some people used to say that she had a big secret that no one knew.

That day she got up, showered and dressed then went to the library. When she got there, she saw some children and then she got a phone call. 'OK,' she said and put the phone down. Then there was a man that came in. She followed every move that he made, he got a book and took it up to the desk and Mary stamped it, still watching him. After that Mary made a phone call, she dialled 15 100 15. She was talking about the stuff that the man had done.

That night Mary went to an old building, knocked on the door and the door opened. There was a man with a badge on which said *Undercover police*. They stayed in the house for about two hours and then Mary came out and went back home.

The next morning, Mary was at the library, like every day. Mary was waiting for the man to come because he had to return the book. In he came and gave Mary the book. He looked at the other books, Mary was watching him, he took a book, walked slowly to the door but he was too slow. Mary got him, '*Undercover police,*' she shouted. 'I am taking you to jail for stealing,' she said. Everyone's mouths were wide open with shock, they couldn't believe it! She phoned the police to take him away. He went away and was never seen again. Mary went on doing more things for the police and caught lots more criminals.

Lisa Rae (11)
Newhills Primary School, Aberdeen

THE HAUNTED CASTLE

My horror begins on a cold, wet night, in late December. It must have been the worst thunderous and violent night I have ever come across in my life. The road was drenched in deep puddles of water, overflowing the drains. My mum was getting very disturbed by the amount of water on the road. My mum said, 'The next house or inn we come up to, I'm going to ask for some accommodation overnight until the storm clears up.'

We drove for ages in the dangerous flow of water until we came to a large, dark, gloomy castle. My mum looked so relieved and her whole face lit up with joy so we got out of the 4x4 and basically swam to the door.

The castle was full of creepy gargoyle statue things that sent shivers up my spine. They were ugly things, with long snouts and baring teeth, it's enough to make anyone feel insecure. My mum rang the bell eagerly to see if there was a reply. As the door opened, it began to creak like an oak blowing in the wind. A small ugly figure appeared, 'Can I help you?'

I began to explain to him how we needed shelter overnight because of the storm. He brought us inside as the door slammed behind us, leaving an echoing sound in my ear. 'Make yourself at home,' he said, 'my master will be with you shortly.' The place was lit by candlelight and there were loads of scary suits of armour around the hall.

My mum and I were fed up waiting so we began to explore. We could hear the floorboards creak every step we took. Suddenly the sound of clanging metal began, we immediately jumped and turned round in unison to the sound but nothing was there. We proceeded along the hall being very cautious. I heard a great scream down the hall and I ran to see. I turned a sharp, narrow corner, my heart began racing as I saw a tall headless figure with his head under his arms. He was covered in armour and bleeding at the neck. I froze, still and scared. I ran, ran like I've never ran before. I screamed to my mum as the headless figure began to approach out of the darkness, 'Get out of here!' We both ran to the door, leapt into the car and drove off into the blackness of the night.

Steven Scobbie (11)
Newhills Primary School, Aberdeen

THE SHORT CUT

The night was dark, damp, cold and misty, as I left the library after hours of studying. Although I was wrapped up warm I still felt a chill in my bones and there was an eerie feeling to the night. The mist was so thick I could barely see in front of my nose. I decided to start my trek home.

My imagination was running wild, with every sound I jumped. The wind whistling past my ears, the leaves rustling and the trees swaying. I was looking at the ground because of the stinging rain and the freezing wind hitting my ice-cold face. I was walking so fast and ruthlessly that I hit everything in my way. I was on my way home. Then I hit somebody or something that forced me to fall back a couple of feet. I got up and looked curiously around, there was nothing there!

I had reached the short cut through the dark and dingy forest. I decided to be brave and take the short cut because I just wanted to be home. I was shuffling along, lost in thought, when somebody scuffed the back of my head. I turned sharply and heard a hoarse whisper in Latin, which freaked me out! I started to pick up my pace because I was scared out of my wits. I was walking fast and cautiously looking over my shoulder every now and then. I couldn't hear it at first because of the wind howling through the trees and twigs crunching beneath the feet. But I definitely heard them everywhere, voices whispering in a different and terrifying language. I realised it was the same horrible hoarse voice everywhere. I turned and I saw nine black-cloaked figures with devilish grins, shining red eyes, and long bright silver swords. But they didn't have any hands! They came charging furiously at me. I jumped into a bush and hid.

I kept wishing I was in my worst nightmare and my mum would wake me up, but this was real life! I peered out of the thorn bush, hearing the clank of metal behind me I sprang from the bush and bolted up the muddy path. Every step seemed to take forever. The glow from the red eyes burned all over my body, while nine shining blades swung all around me. I escaped around the last corner and came face to face with myself, my heart pounded. As I stared in horror I noticed that I could see through him.

As I waited for one of the creatures behind to pierce the long sword through my back, it happened! He came rushing at me, his skin drooping from his bones. I dodged to my left and he completely missed me. I sped up the road with ten ghosts in hot pursuit. I was almost out. A swoosh to the left of me was followed by a sharp stinging pain across my back. I felt the blood trickling down my back; I wanted to fall to the ground and cry. I heard a high-pitched scream, I span around and the ghosts were gone.

I was out of the forest, my nightmare was over. I was shaking with fear, I thought I'd never stop. This was a night not to remember but I think I always will.

Derek McKechnie (11)
Newhills Primary School, Aberdeen

THE TWIST AT THE END

'Oh you are hurting me,' said Sam.
'It's not my fault we have to go home this way,' complained Emma.
'Aargh help me!' Sam screamed.
'What's wrong Sam?' pleaded Emma.
'I've fallen down a trap door,' Sam exclaimed.

Emma tried to find a way to get Sam from the thing that took him. She found a way in and saw her friend in a cage with lasers holding him in so he couldn't move. There was a man with a strawberry shaped face and a water melon body. He looked really peculiar. He was sleeping so I pressed the button and let Sam out, we sneaked out and ran home. We told my mum about the man and she said, 'He is an escaped lunatic that is mad on lasers and buttons. Never go there again!'

Emma and Sam went to the police and told them where the lunatic was hiding out. They went and got him and took him to jail. Both Emma and Sam got a medal from the Prime Minister.

Hayley Mair (11)
Newhills Primary School, Aberdeen

There's No Way Out

'Help me aarrgghh.'

'Cut,' bellowed David, 'You need to work on the scene a little more, that's all for today.'

The four of them packed away the scenery. It must have been ten at night before they were finished. Helena walked up the stairs, the creaks and noises came from the stairs, well that's what she thought.

She crept into a large bed that felt like it had never been used. She closed her eyes and tried to get to sleep. Around half an hour later, she opened her eyes, she felt a hand touch her face. She sat up immediately. She thought she was imagining it so she went back to sleep.

The next morning she woke up and looked at her clock on the shelf, it was 6.43am. She got up and had her breakfast.

'Morning,' Mike said as he opened the food cupboard door.

'Morning, did you have a good night's sleep?' asked Helena.

'Yeah perfect,' replied Mike. 'I'm going to have a bath.'

'OK.' Helena went towards the closet door, she took out a towel with pink and purple embroidery on it. *Whoosh*, the shelf came flying off. Judith went down to pick it up. She handed it to Helena.

'Thanks,' Helena said thankfully. 'Look,' Helena gasped but Judith walked off. Helena stood up, she caught a glimpse of gold metal. She saw that the other shelves were slack, Helena took all the shelves off.

'Mike . . . Mike,' she shouted, like she had found treasure.

'What is it?'

It was a door.

Mike turned the handle, the door was stiff to open, the door swung open with a heavy push. The smell that came out of the room was like sour cheese and something dead. They both held their noses as they stepped into the room. They both peered into the cupboard room. A skeleton stared back at them. Helena screamed and they both turned round to get out, but . . . there was no door! *Aarrgghh!*

Alison Fraser (11)
Newhills Primary School, Aberdeen

HARLAW ACADEMY

One cold day in autumn of the year 1968, in a gloomy haunted Academy named Harlaw, Stephanie and her dad Charles were going to a personal private parents' evening. As Stephanie and her dad approached the deserted car park a sudden blow gushed past them lifting all the leaves and crisp packets off the ground.

Charles cautiously went to grab the door handle when a sharp *greetings* come from the dark doorway and a figure stepped out of the gloominess.

'Won't you step this way,' said Stephanie's teacher, Mrs Milne.
'Are you sure it's tonight?' said Charles to Stephanie.
Stephanie replied, 'I think so,' with a look of puzzlement upon her face.

Mrs Milne showed them into a room at the end of a corridor, which was always locked. She opened the door and it was very creaky. Stephanie was scared. 'This way,' Mrs Milne said.

They went inside and never came out again. The room is locked till this day and no one knows what happened to Stephanie and her dad, that autumn night in 1968.

J Wallace-Mennie (11)
Newhills Primary School, Aberdeen

THE LIBRARY OF DOOM

The librarian stood trying to open the huge creaky door. No one has ever heard her speak. Every night new people were dared to go into the library and stay there overnight but no one has returned! The huge black gloomy floor was thick with dust and every book was strung together with cobwebs.

The librarian was always skittering around, entering only one room, which everyone entered at their own risk! All was fine until I was the one dared to stay there! I thought about it and I knew it was only a library, so I said I'd do it. I had to start in the tall dark scary woods so I ran as fast as my wobbly legs could carry me! The trees swayed in the wind with only the moon as a source of light!

I got to the door of the library and nearly turned back. The library was still open so I walked in. The librarian said immediately, 'That was a mistake.'

Was I the first or the only one to hear the librarian speak? I went straight to a corner and waited until the lights were switched off and there was a *bang* as the door slammed shut. I was shaking like a leaf. A huge cloud of dust flew across the floor as I saw a tall dark figure move! *Was this the biggest mistake of my life?* Footsteps were all I could hear, starting with a walk and slowly building up to a run, edging closer I picked myself up, I ran as fast as my wobbly legs could carry me.

The first room I came to was the forbidden room and to my surprise the door was open. I slid in and locked the door. I flicked a switch and 'Aaaarrrggg!' Skeletons everywhere, then I heard a bang on the door, someone was trying to open it. I quickly ran into a tall gloomy, wooden closet and waited until I heard the door open, I was shivering out of my bones and I thought I could feel my heart bash through my ribcage! Then I heard a low shaky but very scary voice. 'I know you're in here.' As he opened the closet door, 'Welcome to the library of doom!'

Aarrgghh!

Stacey Bowman
Newhills Primary School, Aberdeen

THE CREATURE FROM HELL

It was the night of the planetary alignment and the moon was shining brightly on the roofs of shadowy houses. It was Hallowe'en night and all was normal in Bucksburn. Me and my friends were out guising as usual. I was dressed as Mr Blonde from Reservoir Dogs and Michael and Craig were both dressed as Scream, but what we thought was unusual was that everyone answered their doors and gave us something.

We were walking past the farm road when we noticed a boy, about ten-year-old, who looked as if he hadn't had a meal in months, he was so skinny, playing in the field.

There were no other kids playing with him, he was just playing happily by himself, when it happened. 'Argh! Help, help!' shouted the boy. He was being chased by something and it definitely wasn't a dog. I caught a glimpse of it and from what I saw, it looked like a fox, a wolf or a very large cat.

We walked into the field slowly and cautiously waited for something to jump out and get us, but as we got closer to the spot where he was standing something peculiar happened. He had vanished, nowhere to be seen, not a drop of blood anywhere, zilch!

We looked around the field for half an hour but we didn't find a thing.

'Look over there,' shouted Craig, 'there he is.' We saw him walking down the street as if nothing had happened. We chased him down the road to see if he was alright but he turned up an alleyway.

We went to see where he was and we found him crouching in a corner, not a mark on him at all. 'Are you alright?' I asked him.
'Go away!' he shouted, 'before it happens.'
'Before what happens?' asked Craig but as he said that I noticed the boy was getting hairier by the second, before I realised what had happened, he had turned into a werewolf. He curled up into a ball and started to clench his back as if he was trying to spread wings but then I noticed he was.

There it was standing before me, a werewolf type creature that was hovering slightly off the ground.

'You're a . . . werewolf but you look like a bat with those wings,' I said in a low toned voice.

'How did you get those wings?' Craig asked in a sort of brave tone. 'Did you get bitten by a bat as well?'

'A vampire bat to be more precise,' replied the creature.

He was looking at us in a sinister way, with us staring back at him. He gave a loud howl and he ran straight at us, he was as fast as a bullet and we just managed to get out of the way.

When I say 'we' I meant 'I' got out of the way. There lying on the ground motionless were Craig and Michael. The creature had disappeared so I backed away cautiously. I was about to run but as I turned around, I saw him standing there waiting for me.

I got my mobile out and tried to call the police but he sped past me and caught my phone as he passed.

He slammed it on the ground and with his hairy foot and his sharp claws, that looked like mirrors, he crushed it into a hundred pieces.

It was just him and me now, 'mano a mano', one by one, the final battle. I hurled myself at him but he just flew into the air and back down again.

He gave one great big swipe at me and I was lying on the ground bleeding to death. The last words I heard him say were, 'I must go now and bring my people to glory. You will all perish, you weak humans, ha, ha, ha, ha!'

Liam Neave (11)
Newhills Primary School, Aberdeen

THE INVISIBLE MURDERER

This thrilling story takes place on a cold winter's day in Aberdeen. A man called Doctor Hitachi, who came from China, has recently moved to Aberdeen to start a new job and to be close to his family . . .

Doctor Hitachi's new job is part of a team working on artificial limbs. As a side project he's working on an invisible substance in his lab at his huge house. His son's the reason he moved to Aberdeen.

He woke up the next day to get ready for his first day at Holby Hospital. When he arrived he signed in and went straight into the conference room to meet his fellow doctors. It was a really hard, stressed out first day at work, so when he arrived home, decided he would have a second try of his invisibility substance because last time he tried it, it was really relaxing.

What Doctor Hitachi didn't realise is that when he has this relaxing substance he does things he wouldn't normally do. Tonight he did something terribly wrong. It took a while for the substance to trigger off, but when it did, wow! Watch out! At 11 o'clock exactly he went outside (remember he's invisible and no one can see him). He saw 2 women that were all over the place so he instantly ran over and dragged them and took them into his house. He stored the women in a freezer. Once he got back inside, he fell asleep quite quickly.

When he woke up in the morning, he didn't remember a thing from the night before, so when he looked in the massive freezer, he got the shock of his life. He was really tense.

He didn't do anything, he just stayed calm and went on as if nothing had happened. He went to work and carried on as usual but again after another hard day at work, he got home and thought he would have some substance again. This time he took too much because somehow he wanted to kill his ex-wife for leaving him, he called her round for a nice drink and lasagne. When she arrived she heard the shower on and thought she would make the lasagne because nothing was on. She shouted out that she was going to get the lasagne from the freezer but before he could get downstairs, she saw the women.

Her face went from tanned to pale, then she turned around and on the table, she saw an empty bottle of invisibility substance with skeleton's bones on it saying *Dangerous*. It then clicked that he was invisible and he was killing people.

Her hands were shaking looking left and right, not knowing where he was, it must have been terrifying. She called 999 and said the address and where to come but guess who was behind her. 'Argh!' She screamed, she was drugged but she fell back and smashed into the table and the wine glasses smashed. Dr Hitachi stood on one and cut himself, you could see the blood dripping from an invisible body. He ran outside but the police were there and they saw the blood and shot him in the leg. Just then the substance wore off and they took him to prison. He got 8 years in jail for attempted murder. Luckily the women in the freezer woke up and were OK but just a little bit chilly.

The next day in jail, he said, 'Where am I?' without knowing what he had done.

Connor Rennie (11)
Newhills Primary School, Aberdeen

A CLOSE ENCOUNTER WITH A WOLF

Last spring it was a breezy evening. The sun was just setting in the red-golden sky. It was a beautiful sight. It was getting dark at around six o'clock and my family and I decided to go for a walk. We put on our trainers and jumpers, Dad grabbed the car keys and we drove towards the deep dark woods.

Now, deep dark woods sounds quite scary, and it certainly was. Here is a tale you will never forget!

When we got to the woods we got out of the car. The moon was glowing brightly in the night sky. We walked and walked for a while, but in the distance we heard a small faint howl. We froze on the spot. Suddenly two small and glinting eyes appeared in the distance, but not too far away. We all ran quickly and climbed up a huge tree, the wolf walked towards us and it howled and barked and it scratched at the tree.

I was really scared and wanted to go home. I just wished and wished we had never come to the woods. I was petrified, scared and shaking. I was feeling one hundred per cent uncomfortable. In my head thoughts were mixed and I was in a state of panic. I was thinking, how would we ever get home? Would the wolf leave us alone? I was petrified.

We had a torch with us and turned it on. We saw things that we hadn't seen in the dark, bushes, flowers and the wolf's fearsome white teeth, the dusky colour of the wolf and lots of other things. Shining our torch into the distance we could see a farmhouse, smoke was coming from the chimney so we thought that someone must be in the house, but it was too far away for them to hear our cries for help. We were trapped!

After what seemed like a lifetime, the wolf became disinterested and started walking away. I breathed a sigh of relief. We waited for a short time to see if the wolf came back, but he didn't. This was our chance to escape. We clambered down from the tree one by one and ran as fast as our legs could take us back to our car. Our hearts were pounding like never before and we could hardly talk when we arrived at the car.

When we got home, we were all still trembling from our scary encounter with the wolf.

Next time you go to the deep, dark woods *be afraid, be very afraid!*

Emma Simpson (11)
Newhills Primary School, Aberdeen

A DAY IN THE LIFE OF PC COLIN THOMPSON

One cold, frosty morning in winter, PC Colin Thompson started work at 6am. As soon as he entered the police station, the alarm of the local bank rang out. PC Colin Thompson jumped into his police car and drove to the bank as fast as he could. As he turned the corner to the bank, he saw a man running towards a car parked outside the bank. The man was wearing a hat and a scarf covering his face, he was also carrying a sack. He got into the car and sped off with his tyres screeching. The man has just robbed the bank, thought PC Colin Thompson. Without thinking twice, he hurried after the car.

PC Colin Thompson soon found himself heading out of Aberdeen. The robber went through red lights, didn't stop for people crossing the road and an old lady had to jump out of the way. PC Colin Thompson knew this was going to be a tough one, so he radioed for backup. PC Colin Thompson told police headquarters he was heading north past Ellon towards Peterhead. Their reply was they would set up a road block near Peterhead. The robber was driving very dangerously at 90mph making it hard for PC Colin Thompson to keep up.

About a mile from Peterhead the car sped round a corner. PC Colin Thompson knew the road block was ahead and started to slow down. When the robber saw the road block he slammed on the brakes. The robber's car started to skid. The car spun round on the road and ended up in the ditch. PC Colin Thompson stopped his car and ran over to the robber's car which was stuck in a ditch. He opened the front door and pulled out the robber. 'You are under arrest,' said Colin Thompson and took the robber to the police car. Other police cars arrived to help PC Colin Thompson. Once the robber was safely in the car, PC Colin Thompson pulled off the robber's hat and scarf and found out that it was none other than Joe Blair, a well known bank robber.

'Well done, PC Colin Thompson,' said the Inspector. 'You will get a promotion for this. As for you Blair, it's back to jail for a long time.'

David Shepherd (10)
Newhills Primary School, Aberdeen

A DAY IN THE LIFE OF

While lying on my cosy bed I hear a car pull into the driveway. This is my signal to have a stretch then slowly and sleepily walk downstairs to meet the lady of the house. I like this particular part of the day as I receive the first show of affection. I then make my way to the kitchen where I am served my first meal of the day and I am thankful it's not fish, I don't like fish.

The lady of the house opens the back door for me to wander out and survey my surroundings and see if anything has changed in my absence. Finding everything the same I stroll back into visit the youngest member of the family, who plays with me.

I nestle down beside him and watch TV until 18.30 when the man of the house comes home from work. This is an important part of the day as it is their main mealtime. Seeing them seated at the table, I find to my horror that my dish is empty! It is time for revenge as this happens often. I resort to miaowing until one of them feeds me.

When they are finished I pick the best lap to sit on and snuggle down and watch TV but, of course, this is delayed due to cello practise.

It is then time for bed. I give them long enough to fall asleep then I have some fun by waking them up for water then downstairs for food and once more to go outside. Mission accomplished I am outside, fed and watered. I check for intruders and hunt for food, then at 06.30 a light goes on in the kitchen. I soon make my way back home. I deposit any presents caught (ie a mouse) but I don't know why I bother, they never appreciate it. I then have breakfast and waken the youngest of the house to get patted and pampered.

I wait until they are at work and school so I can have my main snooze until I hear the car pull into the driveway once more.

Christopher Watt (10)
Newhills Primary School, Aberdeen

THE DAY THAT WENT WRONG

The day started badly for Lisa. Wednesday 16th October, the first day at her new secondary school. Lisa woke up suddenly, she could hear someone shouting but didn't know what they were saying. It was her mum shouting at her to get ready because she was going to be late. Lisa looked at her clock and jumped out of bed. Lisa didn't have time for a shower. She got dressed quickly and grabbed her bag. She ran downstairs and grabbed an apple for breakfast. As she opened the front door the bus passed and she knew that she would have to walk to school.

It was ten past nine before she arrived at school. She was told that her first subject with maths in room 12B. Lisa was so angry at being late that she didn't listen to the directions she was given and got lost. The class all looked at her as she opened the door. The teacher told her to go and sit down and gave her some lines for being late for class, the other pupils laughed. As the teacher told the class what to do, Lisa listened but didn't understand what she was supposed to do. She didn't want to ask, as she felt stupid for not understanding.

At lunchtime Lisa joined the queue for the canteen, she just followed everyone else doing what they did. Once she got her tray she looked around for somewhere to sit, she saw a small table in the corner and went to sit down. Lisa sat all alone wishing that someone would speak to her, she wanted to cry.

Her next two classes, English and German, weren't too bad but still no one spoke to her. Lisa was glad when the bell rang and she could go home. Lisa headed for the school gates and her bus but as she didn't know which bus she should take she started to walk home.

It was raining as she walked and it was getting dark and foggy. Lisa decided that she hated this quiet little village where she didn't know anyone and had no friends. 'Give it time,' Mum had said yesterday, but Lisa had made up her mind to hate it all.

She pressed the button and waited for the green man so she could cross the road. Suddenly she saw this lorry coming she turned round and saw the lorry hit a girl on the crossing. Lisa didn't know what to do, but decided to keep going because people around her were rushing to help.

When Lisa got home she went up to her room. She was going to have some crisps and Coke and put on some music to listen to while she wrote her lines, but decided to have a lie down on her bed.

She woke up when she heard her mum and dad come in. Lisa got up and went down to tell her mum and dad about the accident she saw. When she got to the bottom of the stairs her sister came in the front door with a policeman and police woman. Going straight past Lisa they all went into the kitchen. Lisa followed but stopped as she heard the policeman tell her mum and dad how she had been crossing the road when a lorry had knocked her down. She had suffered serious injuries and died before anyone could help her.

Lisa couldn't believe her ears, she tried to scream that she was there with them. She stood in front of her dad shouting that it was a lie. As Lisa reached out to touch her dad he moved towards her but didn't stop. Lisa saw her dad walk right through her. The last thing Lisa saw was everyone crying and then it went black.

Pauline Gordon (10)
Newhills Primary School, Aberdeen

FAMILY DAY OUT

One morning I woke up and remembered it was my birthday. I quickly got dressed, got washed and ran downstairs to open my presents. As a birthday treat I was going to the Safari Park at Blair Drummond with Mum , Dad and Clare.

We made the sandwiches and put them in the car, then we left. I brought my Gameboy and games to play with because it took two hours to get there.

When we arrived, we had to pay to get in. Adults were £20 and Children were £10. After we had done that we parked the car then set off to see the animals. We saw lions, elephants, penguins, otters, zebras, camels, deer, bears, bison and pigs. We then went on the boat trip to see the monkeys. The captain started to throw bananas which made the monkeys appear from the trees. Watching the monkeys eat bananas began to make us hungry, so we had our picnic. My mum had brought my birthday cake and everybody sang Happy Birthday to me.

At two o'clock it was time to go and see the sea lion show. The sea lions were real show-offs doing their tricks. I thought it was a very funny show.

We went to the amusements next and I thought the slide was fun. There were electronic games and rides that I enjoyed too. Then it was time to see what we had been waiting for, the dangerous, deadly, ferocious tigers. We had to go by car and keep our windows shut just in case they tried to kill us. Some of the tigers were having their dinner and the ones that had finished were lying down. We got out of the car and went to the viewing area but were unaware that a monkey had jumped in the car and hid under a rug on the back window.

On the way home there were strange noises coming from the back of the car and we all looked at Clare, who said, 'What are you all looking at me for?'

When we arrived home we got the picnic box out of the boot and all of a sudden the monkey jumped out of the car. What a shock we all got! I begged my mum and dad to let me keep the monkey but the next day a man from the safari park came to take him back. I was sad to see him go but enjoyed having him for a sleepover.

Stewart McIntosh (11)
Newhills Primary School, Aberdeen

WIZARD MAGIC

Hi my name is Cara and this is how my story goes.

It all happened this week when Jade was staying all night at my house. We were sitting talking about what we were going to do the next day. Jade wanted to stay in and play with the computer because she did not have one at her house, but because the weather forecast was so lovely I did not want to play on the computer, I wanted to go to the beach.

When we woke up in the morning the sun was streaming through my bedroom window and I jumped out of bed and shouted, 'Jade! Jade! Wake up the sun is shining.' When we went downstairs to have our breakfast Jade said that she also wanted to go to the beach. After we had finished our breakfast we rushed upstairs to get dressed. My mum prepared a packed lunch for us while we packed our swimsuits, buckets and spades. We were very excited and could not wait to get to the beach.

When we arrived at the beach there were only a few other people there. We changed into our swimsuits and laid our towels onto the sand where we could lie and sunbathe. We then went for a swim in the sea. The water was lovely, clear and warm and when the sun was shining on the water, you could almost see your face in it. We swam for about half an hour and then went back onto the beach to make sandcastles. We built a huge sandcastle with a moat around it, as the sea trickled up beside us it filled the moat with water. A few kids were standing watching us and saying how cool our sandcastle was and could they help build another one. We helped them for a little while and then went to have our lunch.

After lunch we went back into the sea with our snorkels and flippers. While we were snorkelling, we kept hearing a swishing noise under us and didn't know what it was. Jade thought it was a shark but I knew there were no sharks in this part of the world, so I wasn't scared. After about ten minutes, I went under the water to see what it was and I couldn't believe my eyes when I saw a real-life mermaid. I quickly went back to the surface to tell Jade and she thought I was making it up. I told her that I wasn't making it up and if she didn't believe me, she could go down and see for herself.

She swam down and when she came back up to the surface, she was so excited that the only thing she could say was, 'Holy moly! I can't believe it, there is a mermaid down there!'

We both swam down together to see if the mermaid was still there. She was and we started to play with her. We swam round in circles, playing tig and tag. We were having great fun together, but Jade and I had to keep going to the surface to get air. After we had played for about an hour, we said we would meet her tomorrow at the same time.

The next day after we played with the mermaid, Jade and I were sitting talking and we wished and wished that the mermaid could come out with us to the cinema. The next day when we were at the beach a wizard magically appeared in front of us and changed our friend into a human. We thanked the wizard ever so much for making our wish come true. After the wizard changed our friend into a human he magically disappeared into thin air. We ran along the beach with Ocean (the mermaid's name) laughing and playing. Then we went back to my house for a sleepover.

The next day we got up, had breakfast and then got dressed. My mum took us to the cinema to see Crossroads. During the film we had a popcorn fight and after the film was finished we went back to Jade's house and ever since we have been best friends.

Cara Fraser ((11)
Newhills Primary School, Aberdeen

OUR TRIP IN HAWAII

It was the start of our holiday in Hawaii. It was scorching hot. Derek, Michael and I went to see what we could do. When we arrived at the information centre, Michael and I were already arguing about what we were having for supper.

'Well,' said Derek at the top of his voice, 'is it scuba-diving or tennis?' He was being totally ignored. 'Right, scuba-diving.' So we got packed and off we went.

We were raring to go. We had butterflies in our tummies. We went on a white boat lined with wood. 'This is where rare sharks are seen,' said the captain. Our boat was called Silver Streak. The water rippled as the boat sped through the water. The spray from the sea washed our faces. 'Here is the spot,' said the captain.

We dropped off the boat. *Splash* went the water. We swam around a bit and we went further down. As we went down it got darker and darker. We saw what looked like the remains of a ship.
'Let's explore!' said Michael.
'OK,' said Derek.
Michael explored the deck and Derek explored the basement. I explored the kitchen.

After half an hour, I went back to the deck to get Michael. I saw him go into the basement, so I swam after him. He went into the basement. So did I. I closed the door and . . . *crash!* A pole fell down and hit Derek on the head. We swam back up to the boat and Derek was taken to hospital. After two or three days he was fighting fit and we went home to sunny Aberdeen to find that we were front-page news.

Jevon Ferguson (11)
Newhills Primary School, Aberdeen

NEARLY CAMPING

In the forest beside Balmoral Castle three girls called Joanna, Clare and Sarah were telling ghost stories around a fire. Joanna had persuaded her mum to let her and her friends go camping. They had been really excited and could not wait. This was the first time they had been allowed to do anything like this on their own. They had arrived at the forest early in the morning.

The sun was shining and they started to walk around to find somewhere to set up camp. They climbed trees, played hide-and-seek and tig and tag. They lit a fire and started to cook some sausages and beans and that's when they started to tell ghost stories. Joanna told a story first about a haunted castle but the other girls just laughed.

When Clare started to tell her story, it was getting dark. Joanna and Sarah were really scared at Clare's story which was about a vampire. Just then they heard a noise coming from some bushes and a flashing light behind a tree so they went into the tent and the rustling and the flashing stopped and they went to sleep. Not much later, they were disturbed by loud footsteps coming closer and closer. Now the girls were too frightened to go out of the tent, except Sarah. The other girls were saying, 'Don't go out there!' but she did. The footsteps stopped and the next five minutes were silent.

When Sarah came back to the tent, she said, 'There's nothing there.' They decided to go back to sleep but then the footsteps started again but this time they sounded like a giant's.

Joanna remembered that she had her mobile phone with her so she phoned her mum and said, 'We want to come home!' Her mum came and picked them up and took them home. The three girls will now never know what actually happened.

Ryan Linton (10)
Newhills Primary School, Aberdeen

THE MAGICAL CUPBOARD

One morning Lucy woke up to find the beautiful sun shining in her eyes. She lay there thinking of getting up but she didn't, well not for another ten minutes anyway.

She stretched up and got out of her bed, then opened the doors of her cupboard and searched for her new trousers and tops. When she drew back her clothes, Lucy saw a light. It was quite faint at first but gradually got brighter and brighter.

Lucy stood there with a puzzled look on her face. Then she got another big shock as a large gust of wind came and swept her off her feet. The direction of the wind changed and instead of it pushing her away it pulled her into the wardrobe.

The next thing that Lucy knew, was that she was lying on a raft floating down a river, somewhere in another world. Lucy was a little worried because she didn't know how to swim. She tried to sit up but something was holding her down. Something very, very strong. She tried and tried to get up but it was no use. Then something hit her, this all seemed familiar. She took a moment to think and then she remembered that she had seen this in a movie. She would first hear crashing noises and then she would fall over a waterfall and then that's how it would end. Then guess what? She started to hear crashing. Lucy knew what was coming, so she closed her eyes and held on tight to the raft (not that she could do anything else), Her whole life flashed before her, but then her thoughts were interrupted by a sound that sounded like a fishing rod.

Then it happened again, the gust came and lifted her up into the sky. Then she found herself sitting in her class doing her maths, but she wasn't doing maths, she was marking the maths like her teacher. Hang on a minute, she thought, I am the teacher.

To her relief the bell rang for the children to go home. She quickly said, 'Tidy your desks and then you can go home!' When all the children had left she sat at her desk and started to think what to do. Lucy was feeling all sorts of feelings at that moment. After ten minutes she thought of something that always worked, she tried pinching herself but for once in her lifetime it didn't work.

The moment she had been waiting for had come. The gust of wind came again and lifted her up into the air and then disappeared. Then she found herself sitting on her bed with the beautiful sun shining in her eyes. Lucy then heard her mum, Jill, calling her for her breakfast. She stumbled down the stairs, then sat herself down at the table. She sat eating her breakfast, staring into space and wondering whether or not what had happened was all a dream. Then she looked at her wrists and they had red marks all around them from when she was tied to the raft.

She sat back and felt a little breeze rush past her face.

Sarah Ness (10)
Newhills Primary School, Aberdeen

SUPER CARROT

In a month called November there was a carrot called December. December lived in a drain and he had no friends at all but he said he was a superhero but you could guess that wasn't true.

He was sleeping in his bed and as the day went by he decided to go shopping. The short cut which was through the slide and into the smell and then into the main hall. He was just about to go into TCW, the shop, when the nasty neaps stopped him at the door. They said in a very nasty voice, 'Hand over the money Kid, before anybody gets hurt.'
December gripped onto his money but the nasty neaps picked him up and turned him upside down and shook him until they had every last penny and he ran back home and started to cry.

In the morning he woke up to a pile of money, which he had been dreaming of that night. He wondered if it could be magic or maybe black magic, but that was guessing and he needed to think, not guess. As he washed the marks from his face and got dressed and brushed his hair and teeth, he was beginning to think a bit clearer. He's not a silly carrot nor a smart carrot but he's a bit of a weird carrot, if you know what I mean. Now he's a rich weird carrot. Now he would be a happy person and do what he liked. He could now start to plan his future and what a future it would be. He would be able to get rid of his old life and start a fresh new life.

First of all December needed to find a house. One with a very big shower where he could be clean and smell-free and hopefully begin a new life with new friends and have a family to share his good fortune and he would share it with those more unfortunate than himself. December was very laid back and friendly and he like to be liked by the vegetable clan but there was something missing. I mean where did the money come from? One million pounds doesn't just land on your bed. Where did it come from? How did it get there? There were a lot of questions to be answered.

December went on with his life. He loved everybody, but as I said before, he was still missing something. At nine o'clock at night he was quite tired so he fell asleep. He woke up about one o'clock and noticed a woman carrot running on her tiptoes putting a suit down on the end of his bed. It was a suit with the letters SC and a note that said, *S stands for super and C stands for Carrot and just in case a helmet with your name on it.* They soon got to know each other. Flick was the woman's name. She was in 'Saver X' a gang of superheroes. They needed December to be the leader of the heroes. She explained to him that a man named Doctor Laboratories was planning to take the world over and December was the only one that could stop him from doing it. He finally understood what she was saying so he met the six members of the gang and they were all very pleased to see him. He suddenly felt the part that was missing had been cleared up and that was when he realised he was born to be a superhero.

He went on a quest and on a rocket. He went to the moon and found Doctor Laboratories and his secret laboratory in the middle of the moon. With Flick, the other super carrot, he entered the secret laboratory and saw an evil potion being put in a giant laser beam which was aiming for Earth.

Super Carrot could not stand there looking at his home planet being destroyed so he went on a search for Doctor Laboratories. He saw him talking to the nasty neaps. It was then that December realised he should face his fears and put the nasty neaps into soup and turn Doctor Laboratories into a clown. He ran in and said, 'If anybody is going to save the world it will be me.' That got him into more trouble, he was near a boiling pan of hot soup with Flick and he soon got an idea. He whispered his idea to Flick and they tried it out.

Flick ran off the right side of the wall and December ran off the left side of the wall and they kicked the nasty neaps into the soup. They then went to the main part of the laboratory, where they saw the evil Doctor Laboratories about to press the big red button, which would shoot the laser beam.

They shot in through the door and became invisible. They turned Doctor Laboratories into a clown and grabbed the laser from him. It was a miracle and Flick pointed the laser to outer space and shot it.

Super Carrot went back home and told the story of him and Flick saving the world.

Flick and December got married and had two baby carrots and they lived happily ever after.

Nicole Burr (10)
Newhills Primary School, Aberdeen

DIGBY THE DIRTY DOG

One day in a small cottage near the dumps, lived a Labrador named Misty who had four small puppies. One of them was quite different from the others, he loved getting dirty and his name was Digby.

Digby was always playing with his friend Max, but one day Max was ill, so Digby went to the dumps on his own and got even dirtier than ever. You can imagine what happened next: he got a row.
'Now keep out of that, young man!' said his mum.
'But Mum.'
'No buts. Now go upstairs!'
Digby's brothers and sisters were laughing at him. Poor Digby.

The next day Digby was very angry. He wasn't allowed in the dumps. Max was going to go into the forest this time but Digby refused and snuck out and once again they went to the dumps. This time Digby didn't go home - he stayed in the dumps. Misty thought he was asleep and she didn't check on him and he wasn't missed.

The next day Digby was very ashamed of what he had done. He had been very bad. Misty found him and still gave him a row but Digby pleaded to be allowed back to the dumps and Misty let him go. Max and Digby went straight back to he dumps and they still got dirty. What little Minnie Minxes!

A few weeks later when it was Digby's birthday, they all gave him a mud bath and he got a mud cake which was his favourite thing. Then one night Digby had a very bad nightmare about mud attacking him. '*Argghh!*' he screamed. He swore that he would never go near mud again.

Kareen McLeod (10)
Newhills Primary School, Aberdeen

THE NANNY

A long time ago, there was a boy called Michael who had an illness. The nanny who looked after Michael hated him. Then one day she didn't give him his medicine and locked him in a cold, dark room. There was no light apart from the light coming through the bottom of the door.

She went to the shops and when she came back, Michael was lying on the floor. It was the games room and it was always cold, 24/7. The nanny called Michael's parents and an ambulance. The ambulance people said he had been dead for hours, but the nanny got away with it.

One Hallowe'en night the nanny was driving home and she heard a bang on the roof. She stopped the car and climbed out with her handbag tightly held in a good grip. There was nothing there. The nanny was shaking as if she had seen a ghost. She stepped back into the car quickly and drove off at 90mph. When she arrived home, she was even more frightened than before.

She lived at the top of a hill where nobody goes because it's cold, dark and spooky. She got in the door and it slammed behind her. Then *bang!* she fell flat on her face. She got up shocked and shaking as if she was in a freezer. She ran upstairs and at the very top she tripped over a piece of rope tied tight, as if it was going to snap. It was tied to the banister and a hook on the wall. As she got up she said to herself, what's going on here? Then she heard creaking floorboards so she ran into her room and that's where it all came out.

She admitted that she killed Michael because she thought Michael had come back to haunt her. Then it was all quiet. It wasn't Michael who was haunting her. The bang on the car roof was caused by tree branches and when the door slammed shut, it was the wind. The rope at the top of the stairs was in case someone broke in and the creaking on the stairs was the cat coming up to see her.

The very next day she retired from being a nanny and went to Michael's grave every day.

Kimberley Duncan (11)
Newhills Primary School, Aberdeen

MY NEW HOUSE

Out of the blue, there was a huge bang and the body of Sean Morrison hit the floor with a thud.

Dear Diary,

Today I, Paul Russell, have just moved house with my mum, dad and younger brothers, Douglas and the slightly more annoying, Lee. The house was tall, dark and gloomy-looking. I had the feeling I was a member of the Addams Family. Inside, it was covered with dust and thick with spiderwebs.

I walked in and the door slammed shut. I thought it would come off its hinges. A spider dropped on Lee's head. I giggled at this, but my mum saw me. I went upstairs and entered my new bedroom. It was worse than I had expected. It was dark, the floorboards creaked and the furniture was covered in cobwebs.

It was in this room that I first heard moaning noises. I presumed it was one of my brothers making the noise, but when I turned around there was no one there. What could it have been? I ran down to tell Mum or Dad, but they were nowhere to be seen along with my brothers. I searched all the rooms, but the house was empty. I was alone.

I moved towards the front door and it was then that I saw a ghostly figure in front of me. It seemed to want me to follow it. We wandered towards the back of the house and found an unlocked door. The door led to the basement. As I followed it down the stairs, I began to feel very scared. Upon reaching the bottom, I saw something that made me scream. The bodies of my parents and brothers were lying on the floor. As I turned away with tears streaming down my face, I could see the ghost coming for me. I knew there was no way out.

To be continued?

Matthew McGinty (11)
Newhills Primary School, Aberdeen

ACCIDENT DILEMMA

Last year I was in a catastrophic accident and it ended with me in a terrible coma. I was 12 years old and holidaying with my family in sunny Majorca.

It all started on the way back from our magical holiday. I was asleep in the back of the warm car when there was a loud bang and I suddenly felt the car plummet down a steep hill. There was a sudden ear-splitting crash and the last thing I remember was being rushed into hospital on a crash trolley.

My family said that I was in a coma for four long weeks. They sang, talked and read to me but I was totally oblivious to their presence.

When I awoke from the coma, I asked where my sister was. 'She's fine and dandy,' my mum said. 'She has a blood clot in her leg but she's going to be OK.' I sighed a sigh of relief.

I thought I was back to normality but the surgeon told me that I had something wrong with my heart and had only a 50/50 chance of surviving unless a heart donor could be found. My whole live has now changed forever.

Kirsty Todd (11)
Rattray Primary School, Blairgowrie

THE SLIMY SCHOOL

One dull, dark rainy morning Holly, Ashlea, Ashleigh and, of course me (I'm Kimberley) were outside the main doors of Rattray Primary School. We were playing hide-and-seek. Holly was it. I ran around the back of the school beside the boiler room.

'Here I come! Found you Ashlea and you Ashleigh. Now where's Kimberley?'

'*Aaarrgghh* . . . slimy stuff! Holly come here,' I said.

'What is it?'

'There is slimy stuff all over the place and I saw an enormous shadow which looked like a monster!'

'Yeah and I'm Brad Pitt!'

They all started laughing at me. I couldn't believe they didn't believe me. For the first time ever, we had made fun of each other.

'So much for friends!'

I told the janitor, he went around and had a look. There *was* slimy stuff but no monster. I didn't speak to my friends for three weeks. He got rid of the slime, but to this day nobody has ever seen the shadowy slime monster.

Was the monster really there or was it all in my imagination? You decide.

Kimberley Tosh (11)
Rattray Primary School, Blairgowrie

INTO THE UNKNOWN

I was in my car with my mum and dad. We were on our way to the new house, in a new town, in a new country. I would have no friends.

I hated it as I'd lost all my friends. It wasn't so bad when we first moved here but after I while I started seeing strange things. Mum thought about sending me to a loony bin. I mean me! Julie, Straight A's, nothing ever wrong with me until we moved to this hell-hole, this death bin!
'Mum! Mum!' I shouted terrified. I thought she'd left me.
'Julie! What's wrong? What's happened?' Mum shouted in reply.
Phew! I thought that because . . . well . . . well you would probably feel the same if you had just moved into a huge house!

When I went to sleep that night, I heard a voice and I opened my eyes and there in front of me was a . . . ghost! She whispered to me, 'Hello,' then she started weeping.
I could see a slash on her neck, it was blood!

I saw her every night from then on. Ten nights later I was lost in the afterworld. I was a ghost!

Kayleigh Mustard (11)
Rattray Primary School, Blairgowrie

PLANE CRASH IN AFRICA

It was a beautiful day in May when my family and I were travelling to Australia on holiday. We were flying over Africa and enjoying the view from the window when the plane suddenly crashed into the rainforest canopy.

The captain announced over the intercom, 'Pull your parachutes from under your seats and depart from the emergency exits cautiously.'

We grabbed our parachutes but the panic-stricken passengers ignored the captain's advice.

My family was pushed to the front exit, whilst I was pushed to the rear exit. Separated! I scrambled from the exit, deployed my parachute and suddenly realised my parents were not in sight. My emotions were so strong, I released a scream of horror as I floated down to the forest floor. I was alone. Had they survived? I frantically began my search. I struggled through a bush and to my astonishment, a fierce, ferocious lion was eyeing me up for dinner! Luckily for me, some poachers shot it. I manoeuvred myself through a bush and heard moaning noises. There in the trees were my parents, suspended by their harnesses. I was overwhelmed with joy that they were alive. Now it was up to me if my family were to survive . . .

Colin Pirie (11)
Rattray Primary School, Blairgowrie

SILENT MIDNIGHT

In the magical winter sun, I was in the deep, dark Dundee dungeons when I heard a creak. It sounded like a rusty door swinging backwards and forwards, backwards and forwards. *Crreeaakk!* I walked further into the corridor. I waited and then walked on. Then I came to a dead end. What was I to do? I had nowhere to go so I turned back but, uh-oh, there stood a headless man. *Aargh!* I gulped. Am I going to die? I looked at my watch. Ah, I know why he is here, it is because it is midnight. At five minutes past, he disappeared, but then another one appeared. I am definitely going to die! Oh no I wasn't, there was a door in the wall. But that wasn't there before, I thought to myself. I said, 'You'll never get me now.' You've guessed it - I banged my head on the door.
All went quiet and I thought of the title of this story - 'Silent Midnight'.
I then jumped through the door, legs first. 'Yes!' I shouted in relief.
I don't think I will ever go to the Dundee dungeons alone at midnight again.

Rachel Scotland (11)
Rattray Primary School, Blairgowrie

THE DARK CASTLE

The sky was dark and cold over the crumbling sandstone castle, like a man in a bad mood. Every night there were haunting noises coming from the rusty balconies.

I walked up to the house slowly and warily like a mouse in an open room being watched by a cat. The turrets were mouldy and green. Suddenly, I saw two wide, yellow eyes peering out of a balcony window. I turned on my heels and ran.

I didn't know where I was running to, but I kept on until I rammed into a small fountain that was brewing red liquid. Some splashed on my face and I felt odd and weary. I cried for help. To my surprise nothing came out of my mouth. The only thing that came out of my mouth was blood! The more I tried to speak, the more I spurted out blood.

After a while I thought, why on earth did I have to make that bet with my so-called friends? They are going to be the death of me. Finally, after two hours of bleeding, I ended up as a pile of skin and bone.

Jamie Knight (11)
Rattray Primary School, Blairgowrie

THE TURQUOISE SPIRIT

The sun is setting in the pale blue sky. It looks like an orange equally sliced in half, surrounded in raspberry syrup on a pale blue plate.

A young, mature figure made a silhouette through the sinking ball of orange. It felt like a dream. The girl entered an imaginary door and faded away.

Suddenly, a bright light covered the area, maybe even the world. I walked into the air. I couldn't see where I was going. I felt a warm hand comfort my shoulder. I jerked my head and saw a strange image. Not quite human and not quite anything else, it was a turquoise light. A shiver ran down my spine, but it was a delightfully weird feeling, mixed with emotion.

Screech! A noise came from behind me. I jerked my head again and the strange being was telling me something.
'Do not be afraid. Take three steps forward and close your eyes. Count to five and make a wonderful wish.'
I took the anonymous advice and wished that I was home with everything back to normal. I felt myself spinning and all my worries disappeared. My wish came true. I stood as still as a statue and gazed at the sunset from the start.

Michaela Arnold (11)
Rattray Primary School, Blairgowrie

MY GRANDAD

One evening I had a friend over for tea and we heard a funny noise from upstairs. We went up and there was nothing there, but we were scared. We ran downstairs to tell my mum that we were scared because there was a funny noise upstairs, but she had gone. Then there was another noise from outside. We looked out of the window, but nothing was there. We were even more scared and we ran around the house like headless chickens. My friend started to cry, but then my mum came into the room. I ran to her and said, 'I heard a funny noise from upstairs.'
My mum said, 'It's nothing.'
Then it came again. We were all scared. My mum said, 'Ignore it!'
Tom, my friend, said, 'How are we meant to ignore it if it's in the house or outside?'
Then my dog came in and made a growling noise. My mum said, 'What is it girl?' She took us upstairs and my grandad was in the dog's bed snoring.

Gregor Maclean Lees (10)
St Cyrus Primary School, Montrose

A DAY IN THE LIFE OF A HORSE

It's 6am and I've got 11 lessons to do. This is going to be a hard working day at Commieston Stables. This is where I work and live.

It's now 8am and time for my first lesson. By the way, my name is Jo Jo. The lesson has started and I've got this girl on my back who I've never seen before. She must be new here. I think I'll go easy on her.

Well, that was tiring and I've still got 10 more lessons to do.

The first five were easy, but the other six were very tiring indeed. It's now 7pm and here comes my owner, Debbie. What's in that bucket? Oh, it's my favourite, carrots and apples. What's that in her hand? Oh, Polos, my favourite. It might have been a hard day, but this is really worth it.

Georgina Riley (9)
St Cyrus Primary School, Montrose

THE DAY I WENT KAYAKING

It was the most nerve-wracking day of my life. I went to Stornoway in Lewis. I had put on various layers of sweaty, woolly clothes, which was really annoying because all I wanted to do was get out and *do it!*

By the time I had reached the harbour, my heart was beating like a drum and when I got out of my dad's car, the tension was so high and rising so fast, that I felt I was going to faint!
I greeted the instructor with great enthusiasm and soon, after we had chosen our kayaks, we were off.

It was a beautiful morning, but still the water in the harbour was as choppy as the North Sea. I saw a lot of seals, including a lazy one who sat on a wooden platform floating in a calm bay! Lucky him! I asked the instructor if we were going to go out to the harbour. 'Yes,' he said, 'but first,' he added with humour, 'we are going to go under the pier!'
So off we journeyed, splashing and rocking from side to side, only for me to find that the waves were dragging me violently *towards* the pier! As they did so, I was getting more petrified by the second. Suddenly, I was heading straight for the pillars holding up the pier! As I got closer, I could see too clearly that there were about 20 pillars in total. I steered strongly to the left and whizzed under the pier with only a few bumps and bashes. Phew!

When we (that is me, my dad and the instructor) reached the other side of the pier, my dad's kayak started to fill up with water and he had to be towed to the shore! After Dad's boat had been emptied out, we were off again.

The water was too choppy, so I decided to surf to the shore. To my annoyance, I bashed into the slipway right at the very end! As I got out of my kayak, I was dripping wet! When the instructor, Tim, got out, he was as dry as a baby's skin! Boy - was I jealous!

To complete my fantastic day, my dad and I went home to my granny's house where we were ecstatic to find hot baths, warm clothes, a roaring peat fire and, best of all, my granny's lovely, and I mean *lovely*, pork casserole!

Jamie Gillies (10)
St Cyrus Primary School, Montrose

THE SPOOKS

Christine and Michael were walking along when they saw a house. The door was wide open, so they decided to go in.

When they were in, they heard a scream. It was coming from upstairs. They decided to explore it, so they quietly went up. They looked around. They could see nothing, but they could hear someone walking towards them. In a flash they were downstairs. They were both very scared and when they tried to open the door, they found it was locked. Then they saw a door in the kitchen and very quickly ran to it. They heard a voice saying, 'You will never leave,' and they were very frightened.

Christine and Michael were wandering around for three hours. Just then a window smashed. 'Help us!' they shouted through the window. Some boys were throwing stones.
The boys said, 'Why don't you use the door?'
'It's locked!' screamed Christine.
'No it's not,' shouted the boys.
The next thing they knew, the doors were open and they came out.

Emily turned off the TV and said, 'That was a good film.'

Alice McDermott (10)
St Cyrus Primary School, Montrose

GOALKEEPING

When I hear the voices of people cheering 'Go St Cyrus', they make me feel as if I am going to let a goal in. I stand there and think we are going to lose, but the ref blows the whistle and it's over.

Last year we got through to the final, but Banchory got the winning goal. We were all upset at that moment.

The next tournament was indoors at Inverbervie and we never even got to the semi-final that time.

There will be one tournament we will win with our three fantastic strikers who are Sarah Herd, Alannah Duggan and Emma Rose. It will take hard work to win against Banchory, but it won't take that long to do. We are a good team and getting better each day.

Emma Smith (10)
St Cyrus Primary School, Montrose

A DRAMATIC DEATH

One day I was walking along the riverside when I saw a person floating. I thought it was a boy, but when it turned over I saw it was a girl. She was at my school and I think her name was Natila. I screamed. I phoned the police and then my friend. I was really scared.

When the police arrived, I showed them where the body was. My friend, Kryztine, arrived as well to see how I was. She asked, 'Do you know who it is?'
I said, 'I think it is Natila.'
She said, 'Oh my God, you have to be joking.'
'I'm not positive, but pretty certain,' I replied.
We went home to my house and told my parents about what had happened. They were devastated about the tragic news. Kryztine and I talked about it all night, wondering what might have happened.

The next day we got up early and went to the police station to see if it was Natila, but they told us to go home. We bought a newspaper on the way home and on the front page was Natila, who was declared dead.
The journalist said, 'It was a tragic accident to such a young girl'.

Bronwyn Thomson (11)
St Cyrus Primary School, Montrose

THE VANISHING FUTURE

My name is Margaret Spiller. I shall tell you a story about a strange thing that happened to me . . .

I was walking in Nut Hill Park near to where I live, when I saw something in front of me blocking my path. I ran towards it, curious. Then I stopped dead in my tracks . . .

Lying there, covered in blood and very bruised, was a woman. Her eyes were wide open and it was obvious that she was dead. I stared into her eyes and as I did so, I felt very dizzy. I didn't know what to do. I then remembered there was a phone box nearby. I sped along as fast as I could. I reached it and dialled 999. 'Police, please, at Nut Hill Park,' I said stuttering and then slammed the phone down.

I started to make my way back to where the corpse was so I could wait for the police. I had the shock of my life when I got there. The body had gone, vanished! The police were really angry with me when they arrived. I tried to explain, but they just thought I was mad. Was I mad? Was I hallucinating? I returned home, disturbed.

A year went by and I had almost forgotten the incident. I read the newspaper at breakfast. The headline was 'Woman battered to death'. I looked at the date. Then I realised it was in Nut Hill Park and it was exactly a year since I had seen the body. Had I seen the future? A chill ran down my spine.

Anna Beare (9)
St Cyrus Primary School, Montrose

JOURNEY INTO THE UNKNOWN

'Jimmy, get up right this moment!' shouted Ms Bradwick.

'Yes Ms Bradwick, I'll just be a sec,' replied Jimmy.

Jimmy was nine and had been staying with Ms Bradwick for a year since his parents died in a car crash, and he wasn't enjoying one bit of it! Ms Bradwick treated Jimmy insignificantly, and used him like a slave.

After another morning of terror, Jimmy had had enough. He silently crept out of the garden and ran into the nearby woods. Jimmy was walking along sadly, thinking about the difference between his parents and that horrible old, fat hag of a foster mother who just sat on her backside and made him work all day.

Suddenly, Jimmy smelt burning pine and went to investigate. He couldn't believe his eyes when he saw a burnt, red-coloured, cigar-shaped spacecraft. Outside the craft, standing silently, was an ugly little space life form. Jimmy was intrigued. He walked slowly towards it, with no fear. Although Jimmy could hear no words being said by the creature, in his head he could hear the words, 'Welcome, don't be afraid.'

Jimmy felt warmth and love coming into his heart. Slowly, the alien held out his hand. Jimmy placed his into it, they turned together and slowly walked towards his spacecraft.

Robbie Sharp (10)
St Cyrus Primary School, Montrose

A MARTIAN'S REPORT

My first impressions were that Earth was very strange and a different colour from our planet. I met some humans called Peter and Gran. They were a very strange shape and size. They seemed very nice. Gran knitted me a strange woolly thing she called a jumper. It kept me warm because it was very cold on Earth. The food was very interesting. It had a lovely flavour.

They had an entertainment box they called television or TV. I watched something called 'Top of the Pops'. It had something to do with people singing and music.

We went to something called a fête. There were a lot of humans. They were poking me and weren't as nice as Peter and Gran. There was a creature Peter called a dog. A big, red, very wet and rough textured strip came out of its mouth and it licked me. There were a lot of creatures like it around. A fête must be when creatures and humans bond.

After the fête we went to Peter's house. After some lovely tea and biscuits, I waved farewell to Peter and Gran and left.

Aaron Emery Haake (11)
St Cyrus Primary School, Montrose

THE GHOST OF COSTON CASTLE

The Robertsons were having a wonderful time in England. Lisa was the oldest child at 12, Mel was 10 and little Megan was 5. Their mum, Kate, woke them up early because they were going to Coston Castle. The castle was on top of a hill, about 20 miles away from their hotel.

It was raining when they arrived in Crediton at 10 o'clock. The castle was free to all visitors, but nobody was there today. As they walked into the old, dusty hallway, the door slammed behind them. There was something spooky about this place that Mel did not like. You could see that Megan was scared because she was cuddling her mum and chewing her toy rabbit's ears.

Suddenly, they heard a strange noise like keys in a lock. Lisa pointed and shouted, 'Look!'
There was a light coming from round the corner. They could also hear footsteps coming towards them. Then they saw the silhouette of someone. Megan screamed and hid behind her mum.

It was the caretaker. 'Sorry, the high winds and rain have made the castle unsafe,' he said, 'so we are closed today.'

As they were leaving, Mel turned to thank the caretaker . . . but he had vanished!

Kirsty McMillan (11)
St Cyrus Primary School, Montrose

ROBBERS

One morning I was having a nice dream about my friends from Ireland coming to stay. We were having great fun playing and dancing. I was learning dances and listening to music. Then there was a loud *bang!*

I woke up and my wardrobe, my chest of drawers and TV were all gone. I heard another *bang!* This time it was louder. It was coming from downstairs. I knew it must have been robbers. I got up and there were footsteps and speaking. I locked myself in the toilet in case they tried to kidnap me. At last I plucked up the courage to go down.

I saw them, they were taking everything away. Then I thought, where are my mum and dad? Had the robbers taken them away? Were they hiding? I had to find them quickly. I looked in their bedroom, everything was gone. I wondered where they all were. Then I remembered we were moving and they were the removal people!

Sonia Brownlie (10)
St Cyrus Primary School, Montrose

MY FAMILY

We're the Pryce family and we live at 47 Newton Gardens in the quiet little town of Shalton. I'm Ben, the youngest member of the family, and there is Tom who at 9, is two years older than me.

Life in our house is really chaotic. I usually just sit and watch them in amazement, as it's the same thing every day. I escape to the garden to find some peace. I like to sit quietly watching all the birds that come into the garden to eat from the bird table that Dad built.

When Mum comes to hang out the washing, I like to help by carrying the peg bag for her. My favourite time of day is after school as Tom and I play football together in the garden, or sometimes down at the park. We often go for a run down by the river if it's a nice day.

After all the exercise, I like nothing better than to lie on the couch and have a nap. Even with all the noise around me, I can just close my eyes and sleep through anything. After all, seven is not that young for a dog!

Ragan Smith (9)
St Cyrus Primary School, Montrose

The Day I Met Spyro

One day I was playing my PlayStation game Spyro and I pressed a button and a great flash of lightning struck me. I appeared in my PlayStation game. I looked in a water reflection and came up as a dragon like Spyro, but pink, with the name Sassy.

Suddenly my sister came into the room, picked up the remote and was working Spyro. Her friend Avril came in and worked *me*! I explored and met all the characters and challenged Spyro in a race. The winner got twenty jewels and an orb.

We raced through sunny beaches and swam through and underwater. After an hour Mum called Nicola and her friend Avril to tea. I started to get to know Spyro better and asked him what it was like to be in the life of Spyro and he answered, 'Fun!'

Suddenly I appeared with a flash of lightning in my room and took out the game from the drive. What I saw was Spyro wink at me . . . and that was the day I met Spyro!

Sarah Dunbar (10)
St Cyrus Primary School, Montrose

???

It was the night of the power cut and all was dark. I was sent down to the cellar to fetch some candles.

As I opened the door it creaked. I walked down into the deep, dark cellar and opened the cupboard that we stored the candles in. As I was then flicking the dust off one of the boxes I heard footsteps, then a constant whisper saying, 'You will die!'

I froze but then picked up my courage and stood in front of an old cracked mirror, saying, 'I'm not scared.' I said this three times and then *screamed!* There was a man or something, with slime running off him and he had chains on. I turned round but nothing was there. *It must have gone* I thought. But when I turned round again the thing was still there. I made a break for the door but it was locked. I saw an open window and scrambled out of it. I ran into the house where my dad was standing. He said, 'Where are the candles?' I just stared.

Claire Mottram (11)
St Cyrus Primary School, Montrose

A DAY IN THE LIFE OF NEIL ARMSTRONG

It was July 20th and in two hours I was about to be the first person ever to walk on the moon. To me the time was just flying past. It was half an hour away before blast-off. The butterflies were doing cartwheels in my stomach. I explored the shuttle before I went. It had all seemed to have changed to me but it had not really. It felt very weird. Before I knew it they were calling for me. I was in my suit, carrying my helmet, pacing back and forth. I left to go. I was in the air shuttle. All I could hear was, '10, 9, 8, 7, 6, 5, 4, 3, 2, 1, blast-off!'

It took two days to get there. I had arrived. My heart was beating faster and faster. I picked up my flag, took five steps and jumped down. This was the most exciting and extraordinary moment in my life. And then I said the proudest words I have ever spoken. I said, 'This is one small step for man and one giant leap for mankind.' That was the day I treasured.

Katie Shepherd (11)
St Cyrus Primary School, Montrose

A DAY IN THE LIFE OF RACHEL STEVENS

It is 6.30am and I'm in LA. We are just about to film LA 7. We are going up to the woods because we are filming a series where we get lost and run out of petrol. So, me, Tina and Paul have to go in to the woods in the dark. We say goodbye. We will see them soon. We have to go now. OK I'm in the woods in about five minutes. I'm about to film, 10, 9, 8, 7, 6, 5, 4, 3, 2, 1, action! One hour later we have finished the last ever series of LA 7.

I'm at the airport now, just about to get on the plane to go back to Britain. We get our own plane. I'm on first. Twelve hours later I'm in Heathrow airport. I'm off the plane but I can't believe I was in America today. I'm going to my house now to get some sleep. I will see you tomorrow.

Alannah Duggan (10)
St Cyrus Primary School, Montrose

AN ALIEN IN MY BACK GARDEN

One sunny morning it was the day Neil Armstrong was going to walk on the moon. We were inside watching the news. It was time for the countdown. All we heard was five, four, three, two, one, blast-off. They said it would take two and a half days to get there. 'Off they go!' said the news reporter. All we heard next was some shooting sounds, then a scream, then a big bang in the back garden. We rushed outside to see what it was. 'It's a spaceship!' said my little brother.

Cody, my dad, carefully lifted up the lid. 'It's an alien!' screamed Mum. She ran up to her room and shut her window. She began biting her nails very short and very fast. The alien was green with googly eyes and weird feet. It was very funny and it was trying to get out but it tripped and fell. Mum came down the stairs and looked at it. She thought it was cute. After a while we gave it some food. It liked the food so we gave it some more. The next day we decided to keep it and show the whole family our new pet.

Jenna Thomson (10)
St Cyrus Primary School, Montrose

HOUSE ON HAUNTED HILL

It was a horrible day when me and my brothers, Fish and James stumbled across an unusual house on a huge hill. Fish said, 'I want to go and take a look.' James agreed, but I didn't. Fish said, 'Let's go for it,' and they dragged me up the hill.

We were exhausted when we got to the top. We went in. It was really dark. We heard a noise coming from upstairs, getting closer and closer. It was a big, dark brown werewolf. We all ran as fast as we could into a room. But it was worse in there, there were heads everywhere. Then something crawled out from the dark. It looked like a huge worm and it disappeared through the floor! We all ran out of the door, past the werewolf and down the hill, back to our house.

Christopher Reid (10)
St Cyrus Primary School, Montrose

DESERT DESPAIR

In the summer holidays, Lucile and Richard were going away on a camping holiday in the Sahara desert. Lucile had golden hair, it was about shoulder-length. She was ten. Richard had black, spiky hair and wore round glasses. He was thirteen. They had been driving for two hard hours.

'We are here at last,' Mum said. Finally they'd arrived in the Sahara desert.
Suddenly they realised they had no water. 'We will go and find a lagoon, won't we?' encouraged Richard. So they walked, feet sinking into the scorching sandy hills. 'Look' Richard pointed as they saw a wide, round lagoon with people around it.
'Wait, it's probably a mirrr . . .' Too late. Richard had jumped right in.
'Yuck!' Richard had a mouthful of sand.
'Told you it's a mirage,' Lucile raged.
'There's one, I bet that's real!' boasted Richard.
'No, it'll be another mirage Richard, let's go back,' Lucile said in a tired voice.

In the end they found water in what they thought was a mirage. Boy, this was the best holiday ever.

Caitlan Wolsey (10)
St Cyrus Primary School, Montrose

A DAY IN THE LIFE OF A BLUE BIRD OF PARADISE

Hi, my name is Rainbow. I live in Papa New Guinea and Australia. It's time to go and hang upside down to attract a mate. I have found one, she is cute. *Oh no, run, people!*

This tree is a good place to hide. I see them, they have guns. I am scared. *They've got me, help!* I am in a net. I am travelling. We have stopped. Now they're letting me out. I am in a cage. Hmmm, birdseed and water. There are a lot of people here. Somebody has dropped a bag. I wonder what's in it, popcorn.

I think I can get through those bars. Yes, I can, I am free now. Maybe I can free the other birds. But how? If I could get the keys I could free them. There they are. I have got the keys, I can free them.

Laura Rana (9)
St Cyrus Primary School, Montrose

NEW STAR DAWNS

Every night an old man called Albus Bell watched the stars through an old telescope. He was a quiet man who kept himself to himself. People thought he was a bit strange, but he was just fine.

While Albus was away one day at a science shop in the city, vandals wrecked his house and broke the telescope. The place was a pigsty, in fact that is an understatement. When Albus came back he was outraged and called the police immediately.

When they arrived they searched carefully and eventually found fingerprints on the telescope. Albus was delighted. Back at the police station they were able to find a match for the fingerprints and knew who had done the act. The vandals had been busy around that area for sometime and had committed several similar crimes.

The town clock was chiming midnight while Albus was watching the stars for the first time in weeks. Suddenly a star appeared in the sky. Albus named it the Bell Star, as he had been the person who had first discovered it.

The vandals were doing many hours of community service after being caught. Meanwhile Albus was famous, everyone in the country knew of him.

Campbell Anderson (9)
St Cyrus Primary School, Montrose

HAPPY BIRTHDAY!

The day my best friend, Willow, was declared dead I was at my 14th birthday party. My mum had come running in. 'Crystal!' she screamed. I turned around and looked at her running towards me. Everyone was staring. 'It's Willow's mum, she's just had a call. They've declared Willow officially dead.' Mum blurted out. I stared in disbelief. I ran out of the room and cried. I'd never had any real friends before Willow.

A week later I was in my room looking through our photos, when I decided to go on the computer. I got up to put them back, when I looked out of the window. I saw something that made me run out of the door. What I saw was Willow waving up at my window. As I got out of the door a chill blew, but no sign of Willow.

That night I woke up to the sound of laughter. I looked at my clock, it was half-past one. The laughter carried on. I got up and switched the light on. I kneeled down under the window, lifted a floorboard and removed a bit of carpet. There under the floor was Willow's body, all bloody and bruised. 'Why did you make me do it?' I sobbed.

Rhianne Malcolm (11)
St Cyrus Primary School, Montrose

JEEPERS CREEPERS

When I was walking home it started to rain. I noticed there was an old abandoned house upon the hill. I decided to go up to it. I had a funny feeling about it but I had no choice, so I walked up the hill and turned the handle and went in. I walked a few paces forward then a strong wind blew the door shut. I walked slowly forward with my heart in my mouth.

Suddenly I felt a tapping on my shoulder. I turned round. There was a glimpse of a white thing going up the stairs. I went after it. When I got upstairs there was the most frightening thing of my life. It was staring at me with its red eyes. It had long teeth and was dressed in a long coat. I was as white as a ghost looking at this monster. I ran as fast as I could downstairs. I went out of the door and ran down the road. I got to my house and called the police but it was too late.

Fraser Coutts (12)
St Cyrus Primary School, Montrose

A VERY DIFFERENT WEEK

On Monday the fourth of March I went skiing for one week and skiing was not what I expected. The weather was horrible, it was muddy, cold and windy. It was the day I got a consent form. I ran from the bus, got in the door and shouted, 'Mum, let me go skiing.' My mum took the letter and read the info. She said yes and I jumped up and down but unfortunately I fell.

On the first day I got up at 6.30am with excitement. I shouted, 'Yes!' I'd done everything that my mum had told me to do before I went to school. When the bus got to the school I nearly fainted because I was so excited. When we were strapped in with our safety belts, we were ready to go to Gulabin Lodge. We met a very nice man called Gustav and a woman called Lydia. We got fitted with ski boots and skis but the beginners were in for a surprise. We stayed at Spittal of Glenshee to learn how to ski. We learnt star turns, snow ploughs and parallels.

On our second day we headed straight up to Glenshee ski slopes. After we were registered, we were on the slope practising our balance on snow. Again we did star turns. In the afternoon we went on the dink dink slope. That was harder than I thought. It was icy.

On our third day we went to the Lecht Ski Centre because of the lack of snow on the Glenshee slopes. By the time we all got to the Lecht we had 90 minutes skiing time before lunch. In the afternoon I was much better at skiing.

On our fourth day we went back up to the Lecht because there was still not enough snow at Glenshee. I was glad about this because I like the Lecht better. I had a great day skiing, until I fell flat out in the mud.

On our fifth and last day I felt sad because I knew I was leaving my instructors Martin and Lydia. They gave us another brilliant day. It was sad to say goodbye but all good things must come to an end.

On Saturday 9th March, me and my dad had a James Bond day. We watched all the James Bond movies. We had included *The World Is Not Enough* and *Goldfinger*, plus his number one smash, *The Living Daylights*.

On Mothering Sunday I gave my mum a CD and a card, which was pretty funny. We also gave her a bunch of flowers.

Yet my week was not good but it was the best of my life, so I don't care as long as I was happy.

Arron Dick (10)
St Stephen's RC Primary School, Blairgowrie

ALICE

Wood Home is a vibrant spectacular place to live, where the flowers bloom and the river sings its song of praise to the heavens. But yet it has a spooky side to it. When night falls, evil enters the tranquillity. In the heart of Wood Home lives the Dazzling family.

Alice Dazzling is wild and adventurous, agile, charming and glamorous. Her father is tall, rugged and not very glamorous. Alice's brother Paul, picks on her.

One mysterious night the wind blew strong. Paul and Alice were in their beds listening to a story about a witch called Relica, who creeps around at night in Wood Home. As they listened, Alice was suddenly sucked into the night. As she walked through the moonlight, the river sparkled and Alice smelled the blooming flower, when a burst of pollen went up her nose. She sneezed and the air was filled with colour. Suddenly she came across a sign which said *Relica's Home. Go away!*

Relica appeared and began to chase her. She caught her and took her to her home. 'What are you doing here?' she growled.
'Nothing! I demand my freedom!' shouted Alice.
'Ha-a-a-a-a!'

Alice woke with a start. She'd had a terrible nightmare.

Anne Marie Walker (12)
St Stephen's RC Primary School, Blairgowrie

THE MAGIC CHAIR

One day I was sitting in my swimming pool, when my best friend Struan came across, climbing the beautiful gold trellis in his garden. We swam about the swimming pool, when the plug came out and we were sucked down the pipes. We found ourselves down the pipe, the place was dark and creepy.

Then suddenly a funny cartoony voice said, 'What are you doing down here? Struan, it's me, Marty the magic chair.' Then light shone as a chair appeared. It said, 'Sit on me and say your favourite place in the world.' So I did. I said, 'Australia.' It began to turn different colours. We landed in Australia.

Suddenly, 'Aaarrrggghhh!' shouted Struan
'What's wrong?' I said
'I'm scared of heights,' he said. Then I slid down with Struan not far behind. When we got to the last slide we started to slide down very fast. *Smack!*

Then I heard a voice calling, 'Help!' and people singing.
I called out, 'Struan?'
He called back, 'I'm over here.'
We ran out of the building, jumped back onto the chair and shouted, 'Home.'
We found ourselves back in the swimming pool in my back garden.

Michael Stephen (10)
St Stephen's RC Primary School, Blairgowrie

THE MAGIC CHAIR

I was in my back garden sitting on my dad's deckchair in my private mansion. I have blue eyes and brown hair. I was wishing that the deckchair was a magic chair and I could go anywhere. I wished that I could be a fish in the Caribbean Sea.

Suddenly I was sucked up into the sky and then I was in the Caribbean Sea swimming around. Then I saw a beautiful fish called Steph. She had green skin and red love hearts and I was different colours too. First I was red and then I was blue. I was all different colours. I fell in love with her and tried to get her attention but she played hard to get. Finally I got her attention and asked her out but she laughed and swam away. I was the laughing stock of the sea. I wished I could go back home but I had lost the chair. What shall I do? I asked myself. 'Good idea,' I said I looked around and saw a small green and pink fish. 'Will you help me?' I asked.
'Yes,' said the fish. So we set off in search of my magic chair.

After a long day of looking I eventually found it. It was in a rock. I pulled it and it came out. I sat on it with relief and wished that I could go home. Suddenly I was back at my mansion on the magic deckchair. I got off it and put it away, never to be used again.

Craig Macdonald (11)
St Stephen's RC Primary School, Blairgowrie

THE SNOW QUEEN

The beautiful Snow Queen woke up on the iciest morning of the year. She wrapped herself in her sea-blue fur coat that matched her eyes; she was looking forward to meeting the people of Icyland.

Later that day another Snow Queen, Izzy, came to Icyland and announced, 'My name is Izzy, my kingdom melted and my people died. This is going to be *my* kingdom!' Snow Queen could not believe her ears, she was so shocked. She tried to persuade her but Izzy wouldn't listen and tried to take charge. Izzy punched Snow Queen on the nose. It didn't bleed but it did hurt. She tried to say no but nothing came out. She tried to scream but still nothing. Snow Queen was a terrible fighter so Izzy slept in the castle and threw the snow queen out.

The kingdom was now ruled by Izzy but Snow Queen wanted revenge. She wanted Yeti to come down and take Izzy away up the mountain. Yeti galloped down the mountain and stopped at the very bottom. He searched for Izzy in every house in the kingdom. At last he caught her and carried her up the mountain and threw her into a cage.

Yeti also captured Snow Queen and put her into the cage. 'Ouch!' Snow Queen shouted very loud, 'that hurt,' she continued. Her plan hadn't worked out as she had expected. 'Why did you really come here?' asked Snow Queen, expecting an answer. Izzy just stared into space but there was a sparkle in her eyes. She knew that sparkle from somewhere before, it was just like her mother's. Her mother had died long ago. Could it really be her?

Jordan Bannaghan (10)
St Stephen's RC Primary School, Blairgowrie

My Wicked Teacher Turns Into A Bat

It was the first day back in PS after the summer holidays. We had a new teacher. She thought we were nice and that she was very smart but not as smart as we were. We had planned a few tricks, like turning her into a frog and making her bottom *huge*. But it didn't go as we had planned - it went *better*! Mrs Forsyth told us to make bats for the Hallowe'en display; instead we turned her into a bat.

Terri pulled her wand from behind her skirt, held it in her hand, flicked the wand and whispered loudly, 'Caberthrcoonus.' A flash of lightning and there was now a bat hanging from the roof. We all laughed and took the rest of the day off.

Eventually after a long holiday, we went back to school. As usual Kasia was hungry so she took out her wand, flicked it towards the picnic table, missed and turned Mrs Forsyth back into a woman.

Oh no! We were given detention for the rest of out time in primary school and worst of all, we got our witches' licences taken away.

We now had to return to St Stephen's as normal pupils at the start of the next term. Mrs Forsyth had moved too and she was to be our new teacher there.

Terri Jennings (9)
St Stephen's RC Primary School, Blairgowrie

SOPHIE'S POSTER

Sophie woke up one Saturday morning, she had recently got a Harry Potter poster and it blinked then spoke to her. 'Hi Sophie.' Sophie could not believe her eyes! She quickly got changed, brushed her teeth and hair then ran downstairs. She grabbed a piece of toast from her dad; he was just going to eat it. She hid the poster in her bag and shouted, 'Bye Mum! Bye Dad!'

Sophie dashed to the end of the pier to the fortune-teller Ezmereldi, an old lady who lived in a green and yellow caravan. Sophie and Ezmereldi were good friends. Ezmereldi got a shock when the poster spoke to her. 'I will do my best. You go to the park and come back here in two hours,' said Ezmereldi.

Sophie played in the park for two hours then she ran back to the pier to find out what Ezmereldi could tell her. Harry was relieved that he was out and free of the poster at last. Ezmereldi gave Harry a hug.
'Where will you stay?' Ezmereldi asked.
'Please Ezmereldi, can I stay with you?' Harry replied sadly.
'No, stay with Sophie, she will look after you.'
'I will, I will,' shouted Sophie. They walked home together.

Sophie and Harry had many adventures together until eventually Sophie's parents agreed that Harry could stay forever and become Sophie's brother.

Kasia Doig (9)
St Stephen's RC Primary School, Blairgowrie

METAL GEAR SOLID

During the nuclear war in China, a commando squad called the A-Team were on a mission to destroy Metal Gear. The commandos' names were James Bond, Indiana Jones, Octocon and Sergeant Sean. Metal Gear is a robot man called Soilidus created to take over the world. It was twice the size of a lorry standing upright. Metal Gear was stored on an oil rig in the shape of a hexagon in the middle of the sea.

In the sea there was already a scout army of Navy Seals, they had obviously been on the same mission at that time. The Navy Seals broke into the oil rig's defences and were soon wiped out.

After the A-Team's briefing they boarded a chopper. After an hour they reached the radar of the oil rig so they switched on their cloaking device. The A-Team were now in position to parachute into the water and begin the swim to the oil rig. A patrol came round the leg of the oil rig; the A-Team blasted them and made them whimper. The A-Team continued to fight their way to Metal Gear, killing many of their enemies on the way. They met Soilidus and had a fight to the death. Soilidus killed Octocon so they were unable to fly away. The A-Team killed Soilidus and then blew up the oil rig and Metal Gear's power source.

Some marines picked them up and the A-Team told the marines all about themselves and their special duties, they all eventually all joined forces.

Iain Telfer (9)
St Stephen's RC Primary School, Blairgowrie

BUFFY'S THE BEST!

I couldn't believe it; we had won a trip to meet Buffy the Vampire Slayer. We had arrived in California, at last. Buffy was there, right in front of me, I thought my heart was going to jump out when I saw her.
Franki whispered into my ear, 'I can't believe we're here.'
I said, 'No parents all week!'
We ran over to her. She said, 'Hi, I'm Sarah Michelle Geller. Are we ready to go?'
We rode in her private limousine to her house, it was a mansion.

In the morning we went on lots of rides at the fun park, the roller coaster, the twister, a spooky ghost ride and another ride called T-Rex. Everyone was screaming and waving their arms, it was very noisy and exciting.

Later that night, Buffy told us the most amazing thing in the world, we were going to be on one of her programs with her. It was a dream come true.

When we arrived at the studio, there were lots of cameras flashing. We were given our scripts and had to learn them very quickly. We only had a few lines to learn, as it was our first time on television. We all went to our places and began to shoot the program, it was fab fun! Buffy said we were 'naturals'.

At the airport I was feeling sad because I was going home. However, Buffy gave us her autograph and now I can't wait to show Mum and Dad.

Buffy is coming to stay with us next year. *Brilliant!* Buffy is the best!

Sarah Stewart (10)
St Stephen's RC Primary School, Blairgowrie

HOW I TURNED INTO A GOBLIN

My friend Stephen and I went digging for treasure. Soon we hit something. It was a bottle full of liquid. 'I dare you to drink it!' said Stephen.
As I did, a strange feeling swept over me. I was changing into a goblin.
'Meredith!' shrieked Stephen. 'You've grown three rows of teeth.' He sounded impressed. 'You've got three spikes coming out of each hand!'

A long, dark tunnel appeared in our hole, we slid into it, it was a tight fit. We were in a dark, slimy passage with a glimmering light up ahead. As we went towards it we saw that it was a hall full of goblins.

When we went in, every ugly head turned our way. An extremely fat goblin a few seats away asked us to sit down.
'H-h-hello,' said a very bony goblin across the table, 'and is this h-human lunch?'
'No,' I shouted, 'this is my friend.'

After a few hours, the goblins suddenly attacked us. Stephen hid but I had to fight! Several goblins were slashed by my spikes and I bit a few with my venomous teeth. Suddenly I realised that the fat and bony goblins were fighting for me, but we were hurt and had to run away.
The bony goblin said, 'I'm B-B-Boris and this is my son N-N-Nathan.'
'Charmed,' I panted.

When we got out, we searched for an antidote but couldn't find one.
'I guess I'm a goblin forever,' I said.
'Can we stay with you? We will be outcasts now,' asked Nathan hopefully.
'Sure,' we replied and we all went happily into the house.

Meredith Johnston (9)
St Stephen's RC Primary School, Blairgowrie

ARRGON'S ODYSSEY

Arrgon sighed as he stared into the depths of space. For sixteen years he had been roaming in his Assyrian Mark Twelve spaceship searching for his enemy, Drago, who had murdered his brother. His thoughts were interrupted by a growl from the airlock. His friend, Jenner, threw him the engine status report. 'See that?'

'Aye.'

'That's how much fuel we have left.'

'Your point?'

'The nearest fuel station is Drago's!' she bellowed, unaware she was shearing his Persian rug with her claws.

'Oh,' he replied. 'Please stop, that's an heirloom.'

'Sorry.'

The pilot, Perry, yelled into the intercom. 'Ship approaching!' Perry highlighted the dot on the screen.

'That's a fuelling station, stupid! Drago's!' retorted Arrgon. 'Prepare to board!' he yelled. 'Land on the outer shell and blast in! With any luck Drago will be on that spot.'

They boarded, shooting their way through guards and booby traps until they reached Drago's chamber. Scrat, Drago's sidekick, was surprised. Parts of him hit every wall as Arrgon continued firing. Jenner caught Drago, clawed at his face, and as she struck his skull, it split in two! His body cracked to reveal Arrgon's brother! Everyone gasped.

'B-b-b-but you're dead!' Arrgon stammered.

'Scrat organised the whole thing, he encased me in this and made the universe think I was evil. I want to thank you for saving me!'

'Great to have you back! C'mere and gimme a hug!'

'Ugh! Get off, you!'

Alexander Leitch (10)
St Stephen's RC Primary School, Blairgowrie

UNTITLED

Dear Siobhan,

You'll never believe what happened last week at school sports day! I met *Robbie Williams!* Can you believe it? Don't worry though, I'll tell you all about the most sensational experience yet. (I wouldn't want you to miss out on all the fun!)

Our whole school got aboard two ratty old strathtay buses and set off to Balhary House. I'm telling you, that house is amazing, it's not even a house, it's a *mansion!* We go there every sports day, but this sports day I knew would be very special, not only was it my last, I was House Captain of St Luans!

Once we'd arrived we all helped to get the gear out of the back of the bus. Well Primary 6/7 did anyway! They laid it down on the green, moist lawn. I looked around while I had the chance. Lovely trees and fields in front of me as far as my eyes could see. What more could you want? Sports day in a mansion with beautiful gardens to run free on, ah it was a glorious day!

Just then Mrs Donald, our Head Mistress, called on us to come and get into our houses for some games. I called my team and checked they were all there by calling their names off of my list.
'Time to play!' We played with the parachute first with Mrs Keast. It was 'Fabdabedozy', playing cat and mouse and the beanbag game was just brilliant.

Disaster struck as one of the younger boys accidentally 'pinged' a bean back near to the wall. Mrs Keast sent me to get it. I ran towards it, but I tripped! 'Ah, help!' I yelled before plunging straight to the ground. My mind went totally blank. I'd been knocked out completely! I suppose you would after falling head first down a six feet drop to the ground headfirst.

My mind was blank for a few minutes. I eventually woke to the sound of ambulance sirens and the sight of *Robbie Williams* above me. At first I thought it was my imagination taking me for a ride. Then I realised it was real and I fainted again!

When I woke up for the second time, I was in a very large room, lying in a king-size bed with my mum comforting me at my bedside and Robbie Williams was outside playing rounders with St Mary's. My injuries were worse than everyone thought, so they took me in an ambulance to Ninewells Hospital in Dundee with Robbie and my mum in the ambulance too.

I was so amazed with the sight of Robbie, I forgot about everyone else. I couldn't believe I'd been so selfish, so I asked Robbie if he'd come to present the awards at the prize-giving and guess what? He agreed!

It was magical! He kissed me when he presented my awards and he told everyone about our experience and we all got invited to the school where he was doing a surprise show just for *me!*

It was the best, there were lights, decorations and cameras! *He was making a documentary and I would be in it!*

The lights were dazzling; it was a dream come true. Everyone was admiring me for my bravery. Now my wall is full of photographs and posters of Robbie and me. I went to every concert ever on, in the whole of Scotland for free! Robbie became not only my idol, but also my friend.

Now you know everything about my week. How was yours?

Yours sincerely,

Louise Croll (11)
St Stephen's RC Primary School, Blairgowrie

THE FÊTE

Dear Charlotte,

You will never guess what happened at school last week. Julia Roberts was our guest of honour at a party at the school. Anyway the pupil council had arranged a fête with a raffle, games, cake stalls and they had even arranged a surprise at the end of it all.

The teachers took us to a big plot of grass where we were going to have the fête.

'There you go,' said Mrs Keast, handing the class shovels. 'Now go and dig some holes for the tent poles.'

We all pulled our weight and the fête was ready in no time.

When Julia arrived at the fête (in her own private limo with two bodyguards Dee-Jay and Q) she was wearing a gold and white dress that shone in the hot summer sun. Julia Roberts officially opened the fête and we all had a good time.

Then came the time for the raffle. The three winners would take Julia Roberts round the fête. The tension was rising. Loads of people wanted to take her round and over 5,000 tickets had been sold. I thought I had no chance. I kept saying, 'Pink 136,' to myself over and over again. Then it happened, I could see the words roll off Mrs Donald's tongue.

'Pink 136.'

'Yes, yes,' I said, bouncing up and down. I stopped to see what number she said next.

'Blue 597.'

Ruaridh who was standing about five metres away started to yell out. 'Yes, yes.' He had always had a crush on her. Then it was time for the last ticket to be drawn.

'Blue 631.'

Clare who was standing right behind me started to jump up and down, saying, 'That's me, that's me!' She was jumping up and down, waving a blue raffle ticket.

We were all called onto the platform that was covered in blinding Christmas lights. Mrs Donald congratulated us and we all got a big box of chocolates.

We started to show Julia Roberts all the hard work we had done. Suddenly there was a long silence and five men dressed in black came abseiling off the roof. They were carrying black pistols and threatening to kill us all. Ruaridh, Clare and I ran and decked all of the five men. Julia Roberts thanked us very much and hoped she would see us all soon.

The next day, the president of the USA came round to the school to thank us for our bravery and gave us each a gold medal with a red, white and blue strap. We all thanked him very much and waved to him as he took off in his private jet.

So that was my week. Hope to see you soon.

From your loving cousin, Jenny.

PS: Watch the news on Thursday.

Jenny Stephen (11)
St Stephen's RC Primary School, Blairgowrie

BYE-BYE MARINIS

One dark, blustery night, RP Marini and his brother, NM Marini, took their men and began to bomb India with golden missiles. Thousands of men, women and children were slaughtered, it was a horrible sight. Commando Pilot PA Smith heard about the slaughter, he was not happy, he gathered his men and prepared to capture the Marinis.

Prince Iain of India gave Smith his whole army to command and he took to the air for war. When the airforce arrived at their destination, they parachuted to the ground. They found golden machine guns hidden in caves and began by sneaking up on the enemy over the desert. Smith and his men had to trudge over orange quick sinking sand and many of them died as they began their mission to capture the Marinis.

Commando Smith and his men fought the Marinis in the quick sinking desert sand, and eventually into the caves where Smith was able to capture and kill most of the Marinis men.

After Smith won the battle and the Marini brothers were dead, the airforce returned to India to celebrate the wedding of Prince Iain and Princess Francessca. The royal couple rewarded Captain Smith with £1,000,000. He was a very happy man and India had been saved from the wickedness of the Marini brothers.

Paul Smith (9)
St Stephen's RC Primary School, Blairgowrie